E

for Jehovah

Rethinking the Righteousness of Christianity

Robert M. Price

With a foreword by
Valerie Tarico

Tellectual Press
tellectual.com

Tellectual
Press

Tellectual Press

tellectual.com
Valley, WA

Print ISBN: 978-1-942897-06-4

Tellectual Press is an imprint of Tellectual LLC.

Many thanks to Dr. Valerie Tarico for her Foreword, and to John W. Loftus, Dr. Peter Boghossian, and Aron Ra for their kind words about the book.

Cover art is by Edwin A. Suominen, based on Ivan Kramskoi's 1872 painting *Christ in the Desert*.

Table of Contents

Praise for *Blaming Jesus for Jehovah*

"This book is written by the man most comparable in our day to the great 19th century communicator Robert G. Ingersoll. In it, Price bypasses the usual cadre of apologists and clergy gatekeepers by taking his case directly to the fleeced flock of sheep still caged in their pew stalls. This book will liberate many of them, guaranteed!"

—**John W. Loftus**, author of
Why I Became An Atheist and *How to
Defend the Christian Faith*

"*Blaming Jesus for Jehovah* is a masterpiece of scholarship. In accessible, clear, and plain language it exposes the moral bankruptcy of Christianity."

—**Peter Boghossian**, author of
A Manual for Creating Atheists

"Evaluating scripture from the perspective of an unbeliever, but with the academic expertise of one who learned his way out of belief, Dr. Price illustrates significant problems with the core concepts of Christianity, problems which are remarkably even worse than the fact that there's no discernible truth to any of it."

—**Aron Ra**, author of *Foundational
Falsehoods of Creationism*

"Like Islam's derivative text, the Qur'an, [the Bible's] pages are filled with tribalism, misogyny, animal cruelty, slavery, and slaughter at the hand or command of God, and treating the book as a blueprint for living has caused centuries of unspeakable cruelty. In *Blaming Jesus for Jehovah*, Price shows that trying to separate Old Testament from New—trying to separate Jesus from Jehovah—doesn't solve the problem. In fact, it is impossible."

—**Valerie Tarico**, from her Foreword

Dedicated to JULIAN HAYDON, whose idea it was.

Foreword by Dr. Valerie Tarico

> In Matthew, a Canaanite woman, a non-Jew, calls out, begging Jesus to heal her daughter, who is possessed by demons. "Lord, Son of David," she calls him. But he ignores her. . . . Finally, Jesus tells her he was sent only to the lost children of Israel. She keeps begging. . . . If the image doesn't bother you, try to imagine an American slave or a South African Black having to do and say the same things to get health care for her child. "Please, sir, even the dogs eat the crumbs that fall from their masters' table."
>
> —Valerie Tarico, *Trusting Doubt*

Search the scriptures says Jesus in the book of John. Across America, Bible colleges and seminaries teach students to do just that. But I suspect they sometimes harbor regrets. When New Testament scholar Bart Ehrman publishes yet another bestselling book about the cultural and literary processes that shaped early Jesus worship—carefully analyzing the residue in the Christian scriptures the way a forensic chemist might analyze a crime scene—I picture the dean of my old alma mater Wheaton College thinking, "Drat! I really wish we hadn't trained that guy to search with quite so much diligence and vigor!"

For Azusa Pacific University, also a leading light of Evangelical higher education, one of the big regrets must be training Dan Barker, former minister and now Executive Director of the Freedom From Religion Foundation. The title of Barker's book, *GOD: The Most Unpleasant Character in All Fiction*,[1] echoes a famous quote from Richard Dawkins:

> The God of the Old Testament is arguably the most unpleasant character in all fiction: jealous and proud of it; a petty, unjust, unforgiving control-freak; a vindictive, bloodthirsty ethnic cleanser; a misogynistic, homophobic, racist, infanticidal, genocidal, filicidal, pestilential, megalomaniacal, sadomasochistic, capriciously malevolent bully.[2]

Barker's book steps verse by verse through the Old Testament, painting a picture that leaves few of Dawkins's descriptors open to question, save perhaps the term "fiction."

Enter theologian Robert Price.

If Evangelical seminary Gordon-Cornwell keeps a list of regrets, there can be no doubt that one of the slots is occupied by Price, who, over the course of 35 years as a professor, editor, member of the Jesus Seminar, and blogger, has systematically challenged the dominant Evangelical approach to the Bible–to the point of questioning whether Jesus himself might be a product of the same literary processes that shaped the biblical texts more broadly.

Today many Evangelical Christians assert that the Bible is the literally perfect Word of God, timeless and complete–exempt from addition, deletion, or revision. But Price's scholarship, like Ehrman's, reveals texts and traditions that have been shaped by human history and human imperfections. The two men may disagree about whether the gospel stories are "mythologized history" or "historicized mythology," but their combined half-century of research and that of their peers converges in a devastating indictment of Biblical literalism: Almost everything Bible-believing Christians think they know about Jesus is open to question. In fact, those who know the most about the Bible–how it was formed and what it contains–end up in the ironic position of making the most modest and tentative knowledge claims about the life and teachings of the figure we call Jesus.

A fog of time and distance hides whatever historical kernel may lie beneath and behind the New Testament gospels, but at any rate this kernel was not the core concern of the writers. Scholars now understand gospels as a form of religious literature that was common during the 1st and 2nd centuries C.E. Those gospels, including the ones in the Bible, are not histories, because they were never meant to be histories, but rather are devotional pieces that employed narrative to convey what the writers considered to be deep spiritual truths.

Like the stories of the Old Testament, the Gospels reweave mythic tropes from the pagan religions that predated and surrounded the ancient Israelites and the early Church. Add this to the fact that many biblical narratives are scientifically untenable or morally dubious–incompatible with what we know about love and truth–and it becomes clear why Anglican Bishop John Shelby Spong has called biblical literalism "a gentile heresy" or worse, "bibliolatry."

Why bibliolatry? Because idolatry means taking something made by humans, something meant to represent or allude to divine realities, and then treating the man-made object as if it had the attributes of divinity: timelessness, for example, and perfection. It means making a physical object or a narrow pursuit the center of one's life to the neglect of something greater.

Christian history, like Islamic history, has been plagued by cyclical iconoclastic purges–attempts to rid society of anything that might serve as a focal point for idolatry. These purges focus primarily on the types of religious symbols that channeled the devotion of preliterate people. But the authors of the Bible and Qur'an had no way to anticipate that, with the spread of literacy, the written word itself would come to replace other visual arts as the primary medium representing religious ideas, and centuries after their own time, the primary form of religious idolatry would be book worship–bibliolatry.

Those who claim that the Bible is the literally perfect word of God behave precisely like our ancestors did toward the wood and stone carvings that represented the divine for pre-literate people. In an age of widespread literacy, what better golden calf than a "golden" book?

Widespread bibliolatry might not be such a bad thing, if the Good Book were in fact, pure gold; but it is not. Like Islam's derivative text, the Qur'an, its pages are filled with tribalism, misogyny, animal cruelty, slavery, and slaughter at the hand or command of God, and treating the book as a blueprint for living has caused centuries of unspeakable cruelty.

In *Blaming Jesus for Jehovah*, Price shows that trying to separate Old Testament from New–trying to separate Jesus from Jehovah–doesn't solve the problem. In fact, it is impossible. We can't separate the Good Shepherd from Dawkins and Barker's "most unpleasant character" because Jesus himself won't let us. *I and the Father are one*, he says . . . . *I am in the Father and the Father is in me. Anyone who has seen the father has seen me. I go to my father's house . . . . Do not think that I have come to abolish the Law or the Prophets; I have not come to abolish them but to fulfill them.*

In fact, Price goes on to show that in some ways the New Testament creates a thornier set of moral challenges than the Old. The concept of an eternal, individually conscious soul has emerged during the intertestamental period, which leads over time to Christianity's most abominable teaching–the notion that eternal torture is the fate of unbelievers and a proportional punishment for finite, transitory sins as banal as consensual sex.

By putting the platitudes and beliefs of their time in the mouth of Jesus, the Gospel writers depict (variously) a rabbi, prophet, god-man, or human sacrifice who is utterly imbedded in the first century culture of the ancient Near East and unable to see beyond it. Their Jesus shares their insights about love and compassion and justice–insights that had evolved and deepened in the centuries since the Old Testament stories of Jehovah and the Chosen People were written. But he also shares their blind spots. It is our responsibility as readers to decide which are which.

People accuse each other of cherry picking the Bible, as if the term were an insult. But if we take seriously the scholarship of Price and a generation of like-minded scholars who have shown us the all-too human origins of the Bible texts, cherry picking is precisely the right approach to both Old Testament and New, including the words and ideas attributed to Jesus himself.

Consider, by way of analogy: No parent with a backyard cherry tree would pick every piece of fruit on the tree and feed it to her children. No matter how excellent a tree, some of the fruit is wormy. Some of it is bird-pecked and moldy. Some wasn't pollinated properly and has been hard and shriveled from the beginning. A loving parent culls through, discarding the bad fruit and feeding her children the cherries that are juicy and nourishing.

But when it comes to handed-down ideas about religion–about what is real and what is good and how we should then live–many people don't apply the same prudent care. They accept the authority of the Bible or related traditions, incorporate them into their own lives, and pass them on without sifting or sorting.

Bad cherries in the bowl will give a child a stomach ache at worst, but bad religious ideas can leave a person needlessly guilt-ridden for life or unable to enjoy sex, or deeply fearful of death, or full of judgment and alienation toward outsiders, or even suffering what some call religious trauma syndrome.[3]

Handing down un-culled religious beliefs from one generation to the next not only passes on psychologically harmful ideas, it is tearing apart our world. Today some of the worst ideas plaguing society are ideas that claim support from the pages of the Torah or Christian Bible or Qur'an, for example the idea that children are born bad and must be beaten, or that female sexuality is dirty and dangerous, or that homosexuality is abominable, or that religious outsiders lack morals, or that war can be holy, or that the Earth is ours to consume as we please and that God will simply replace it.[4]

Those who care about truth and love, the wellbeing of our intricate planetary web of life, or human wellbeing within that web–or even our own children–have both a right and a responsibility to glean through our religious traditions to find what is timeless and wise (there is plenty) while discarding the rest. Rather than being used as an epithet, perhaps *cherry picker* should be a compliment, an acknowledgment of discernment, wisdom, judgment, and responsibility.

In actual fact, all religious believers (and nonbelievers) cherry pick their sacred texts or cultural traditions, even fundamentalists, even those who deny doing so. Every sacred text contains passages that contradict each other, or that demand a level of perfection (or cruelty) that is simply unattainable for most believers; the Bible is not alone in this regard. Whether we are Christian or Muslim or post-Abrahamic freethinkers or practitioners of some other spiritual tradition, the question isn't whether we cherry pick, it is whether we do so wisely and well, based on some higher principle that tells us which passages are nourishing and which should be discarded.

But in order to do so, we must begin by looking with honest hearts, informed minds, and clear eyes at what is actually there.

—Valerie Tarico, Ph.D., author of *Trusting Doubt: A Former Evangelical Looks at Old Beliefs in a New Light*

Notes

1. Dan Barker, *GOD: The Most Unpleasant Character in All Fiction* (Sterling 2016).

2. Richard Dawkins, *The God Delusion* (Houghton Mifflin, 2006).

3. "Religious Trauma Syndrome: How Some Organized Religion Leads to Mental Health Problems," ValerieTarico.com, March 26, 2013.

4. "Religion's Dirty Dozen—12 Really Bad Religious Ideas That Have Made the World Worse," ValerieTarico.com, January 20, 2015.

Introduction

> Finally, brethren, whatsoever things are true, whatsoever things
> are honest, whatsoever things are just, whatsoever things are
> pure, whatsoever things are lovely, whatsoever things are of good
> report; if there be any virtue, and if there be any praise, think on
> these things.
>
> —The Epistle to the Philippians (KJV).

I Was a Teenage Fundamentalist! Wouldn't it make a great movie title? And I was! For years I read the Bible devoutly, trying to understand and to apply as much of it as I could, praying many times a day, attending church at least three times a week, not to mention our church youth group and other Christian youth activities.

I "witnessed," sharing my faith with all and sundry–to their considerable annoyance, I might add. While in high school, I learned about apologetics–defenses of the faith–through some film strip. This meant I didn't have to rely exclusively on blind faith! Wow! It could come in pretty handy in witnessing! Taking the fight to the skeptics!

It wasn't long before I found myself devouring any books on the subject that came my way, written by John Warwick Montgomery, F.F. Bruce, J.N.D. Anderson, Edwin M. Yamauchi, Josh McDowell, and the rest. This approach gave me new confidence in my faith–for a while.

But soon apologetics began to have the opposite effect from what they intended. The back and forth of arguments and their refutation made simple faith impossible for me. I came to realize that no historical judgment could ever be more than tentative, a matter of mere probabilities. On balance, the evidence for the reliability of the gospels and the resurrection might seem pretty convincing today. But that balance could shift. Tomorrow I might hear of a new archaeological discovery or read of a new argument that would throw things into a different perspective. There really wasn't any certainty and, worse yet, there *couldn't* be.

Gradually, I saw the utility of critical approaches to the Bible. Form criticism, source criticism, redaction criticism, comparative religion—all these things so hated by the apologists made my beloved Bible much more understandable, but in direct proportion to destroying my faith in its inspiration and authority. I came to understand that "biblical authority" was one of the "childish things" a person had to "put away" (1 Cor. 13:11) sooner or later, and the sooner the better.

This all came to a climax toward the end of my Master's degree in New Testament at Gordon-Conwell Theological Seminary. Without missing a beat, I enrolled in the Ph.D. program in Theology at Drew University, where I received my degree in 1981. My dissertation was on the spectrum of revisionist doctrines of biblical authority among those Evangelical theologians who could no longer in good conscience uphold the doctrine of inerrancy.[1] A few years later, I was pastoring a Progressive, theologically Liberal Baptist congregation and embarked on a second Ph.D. program at nearby Drew, this time in New Testament, completed in 1993.

Around this time, I switched over to Humanism. I irritated some of my colleagues with my sympathetic interest in religion, not as a believer, but as an anthropologist of sorts, studying a fascinating aspect of culture. I didn't want to attack religion in general or Christianity in particular, but I began to accept invitations to public debates and to write books on the Bible and the fallacies of apologetics.

You see, I still loved the Bible, and I could not let the constant distortions and manipulations of it go by without challenging them. Knowing what I knew, I felt it was my duty. I still do. But this does not prevent my recognizing certain serious problems and dangers inherent in Christian doctrine. There, too, I sometimes feel obliged to give my informed opinion. And that is what I hope to do in this book concerning the moral foundations of Christianity in the Bible.

Readers would be foolish to swallow what I say just because I have these credentials. I never forget that, and I hope you won't either. But you would be equally unwise simply to write off anything I say that you don't happen to like. You owe me, and *yourself*, a fair consideration of the arguments I will present. They must stand or fall on their own merits, and it's your responsibility to decide whether they do.

The Moral High Ground

Christians believe implicitly that their religion is not only highly moral in character but that it is virtually (and virtuously) synonymous with morality. They believe that there can be no moral standard without a God to guarantee it, no moral behavior without belief in God and knowledge of his commandments.

Disbelievers are objects of their suspicion, tarred with the labels "relativist," "nihilist," and other vilifications. Most say they would never vote for any presidential candidate identifying as an atheist. And yet, among these sole possessors of the "revealed" morality, there are notable instances of cruelty and bigotry.

I don't think Christianity can get off so easy as to say these are mere examples of individual Christians conspicuously failing to live up to the standards they avow. That does happen, of course, as with adherents of all religions and no religion. What seems clear to me, rather, and far more troubling for Christianity, is to recognize that these morally troublesome Christians (take the members of the Westboro Baptist Church cult, for instance) are *acting consistently with Christian principles* as they understand them.

I use the word "understand," not "*mis*understand," because, as I want to explain in the pages of this book, there lies buried (not very deeply) under the benign and placid surface of Christian theology a ticking moral time bomb. The Christian extremists have heard the ticking and interpreted it as the moral heartbeat of their faith. Sadly, I think they are correct, doctrinally. It is *Christian theology* I blame, not Christians, most of whom have never realized the sinister implications of what they purport to believe.

The Sin of Faith

That "belief" is most often merely a cheering for certain slogans anyway, and their slogans seldom include the Christian tenets I will explore here in *Blaming Jesus for Jehovah*. I am glad most Christians, well-meaning souls that they are, have *not* seen and acted upon the implications of their faith, just as I rejoice that most American Muslims have happily assimilated to the social mainstream and do not take seriously their scripture's urgings to wage jihad on their non-Muslim neighbors.

But I venture to think that it is time to appeal to these well-behaved Christians to rise to their professed standards of honesty, regard for truth, and allegiance to righteousness. They ought to face unflinchingly the aspects of their faith that are incompatible with these virtues. They ought to repudiate these aspects, even the ones that turn out to be fundamentals of their religion.

To begin with an unshakable assumption that Christianity is true is already to sacrifice its virtue, to commit *the sin of faith*. For when faith becomes preferable to the truth, faith has *become* sin, what Jean Pail Sartre called "bad faith." It's the very opposite of what we mean when we say someone is "acting in good faith."

I will maintain that to continue to uphold Christianity–as historically defined–is to act in bad faith and to make a nefarious farce of the whole thing. And this I say not despite my training in theology but *because* of it.

There is an old cliché, "A little philosophy inclines the mind to atheism, but much philosophy inclines one to belief." What if the opposite is the case? The more you think about these beliefs, the less you wind up believing them.

Revelation Ripoff

There are many thousands of different Christian denominations, sects, offshoots, etc., in the world today. This fact alone ought to give us pause. It ought to make us wonder if something is wrong.

If God has revealed himself and his truth to a benighted mankind, and that revelation is supposed to make clear what we desperately need to know, then, pray tell, how can there be such a catastrophic failure in communication? Why cannot the vast majority of those who accept this revelation agree on what the revealed truth *is*, what it says, what it *means*?

These disagreements are often quite bitter, sometimes issuing in bloodshed. They are not mere matters of minor detail. Do you need to receive water baptism in order to be saved? Should one be baptized as an infant, with no say in the matter? Or is it an adolescent puberty rite, as in many Protestant churches? And by what mode? Sprinkling, pouring, full immersion? When you are talking about the precise instructions for avoiding eternal damnation, it would indeed be foolish to gloss over the details.

And the same range of questions and qualifications vexes the supposedly crucial matter of Holy Communion. Among fundamentalists, we have even witnessed a recent controversy over the gospel of conversion itself: Need one accept Jesus Christ as savior only, or as both savior *and lord*? If the former, is it what Dietrich Bonhoeffer, hanged by the Nazis, dismissed as "cheap grace"? If the latter, do we retreat from "salvation by grace through faith alone," relying upon the "good works" of discipleship to save us? It's just not clear. Why did God not *make* it clear?

Of course, many believers "solve" these problems by simply ignoring them, taking refuge in quiet, obedient acquiescence to their denomination's traditional party line. Leave it to the pastor. He's the one who studied these matters in seminary, after all.

But if you probe further, you will very likely find that those clergy have themselves been satisfied with indoctrination. Not that this is much of a surprise, really. After all, isn't the whole point of believing in an infallible revelation—the Bible, the Koran, whatever—that you are absolved from thinking for yourself about such questions? If you had to do *that*, well, you might come to an erroneous conclusion!

And God, we are told, does not grade on a curve. So some avert their eyes, confident that these questions are designed as tests of their faith. Others simply do not care. They avoid taking such "intellectual" questions seriously enough to find them disturbing in the first place.

But there *are* Christians who cannot not close their eyes (in prayer) to these vexing issues or, worse yet, to the huge number of errors in historical fact and of gross contradictions in doctrine that biblical criticism, archaeology, geology, biology, and philosophy have revealed in the last three centuries. Some Christian thinkers have taken this bull (or herd of bulls) by the horns. Conservative apologists have dedicated themselves to clearing up these problems (or pretending to), assuring their faithful yet anxious flocks that all these difficulties are mere tricks of the light, misunderstandings easily dispelled. I daresay they think of their role as that of a bomb squad, expertly defusing dangerous explosives. But I think of them rather as a bunch of spin doctors, mollifying doubters with creative evasions and misdirections.

On the other hand, there are Christian thinkers who are genuinely open to the facts. They realize it is much too late to clip the wires and prevent the bomb (let's say, of evolution) going off. No, their job is one of *damage control*. What is *left* of Christian belief? What can be salvaged? Can there still be a Christian gospel if we can no longer defend supernaturalism? Are there viable options for redefining "God"?

This approach, that of Liberal Theology, is a brand of apologetics, too. What is the difference? I think it is one that may be illustrated by comparing them to surgeons and conservative apologists to Christian Science practitioners. The Christian Scientists believe that stubbornly denying the reality of the terminal illness will cause it go away. The liberal apologists, by contrast, will not hesitate to amputate whatever they have to in order to save the patient, though his life afterward may become very difficult.

My Aim Is True

To the people in the pews

In this book, I largely ignore both groups of apologists for the Bible and Christianity. Likewise, I do not address clergy who literally cannot afford to face the severe difficulties that honest scrutiny of scripture and doctrine present. Instead, I write directly for the people in the pews.

Often they harbor doubts they dare not utter, rightly fearing they will only invite the ire of their pious peers. They may even suspect that the hostility they would garner would denote the secret presence in their accusers of the very same doubts and dissatisfactions!

If you harbor doubts about some cherished belief, you do not want to hear them from someone else, since that would mean there really *is* a problem. Not just in your imagination, which is what you wish it were!

But if you have come to the point that the torture of suppressing doubt is a greater burden than facing the threat directly, this book is for you. Or if you are a believer who is fair-minded enough to admit that your faith can never be honest until you take an unblinking look at it, to see what it is worth, then the book is for you, too. Such readers, I believe, will have too much common sense to let themselves be gulled by sophistry and spin.

This book is for that vast majority of Christians who sincerely believe (or at least accept, if they don't pretend to understand) as they have been taught. Let me stipulate what I think we can agree is the basic Christian position, what C.S. Lewis called "Mere Christianity."

> God created the universe, man, and everything else. He is the Heavenly Father who so loved us that he allowed his only Son, Jesus, to volunteer to make the ultimate sacrifice to save us from our sins.
>
> God is perfect in every way; watches over everyone all the

time, knows our thoughts, dreams and acts, and hears all prayers and sometimes grants them.

God is an omnipotent, omniscient, and omnipresent spirit. That is, he is all-powerful, knows everything that has happened or *will* happen (and, many think, *could* have happened but did not). Yet he cannot be fully known by his creatures.

God is a Trinity: Father, Son, and Holy Spirit, *from* all time and *for* all time. One in three and three in one, forever unchangeable.

The Holy Bible is a true and divinely inspired, thus inerrant, record of God's activities as recorded in the Old Testament, and of Jesus' teachings and acts as recorded in the New Testament.

Protestants and Catholics, for all their serious disagreements at very many points, agree on these. For example, these words on biblical inspiration come from the introduction to the declaration, "Dominus Iesus," issued by the offices of the Doctrine of the Faith, 6 August 2000:

The Church's tradition . . . reserves the designation of inspired texts to the canonical books of the Old and New Testaments, since these are inspired by the Holy Spirit. Taking up this tradition, the Dogmatic *Constitution on Divine Revelation* of the Second Vatican Council states:

"For Holy Mother Church, relying on the faith of the apostolic Testaments, whole and entire, with all their parts, on the grounds that, written under the inspiration of the Holy Spirit . . . they have God as their author, and have been handed on as such to the Church herself." These books, "firmly, faithfully and without error, teach the truth which God, for the sake of our salvation, wished to see confided to the Sacred Scriptures." [2]

Creed in Crisis

A theological train wreck

One can challenge and debate many aspects of these basic tenets, and over the centuries many have done so–Christians and their opponents alike. It is well worth doing.

But that is not the task of this book. Instead, I will take these beliefs as they stand and inquire after the implications of all of them being upheld together. To be clear at the outset, I believe we will find an incurable conflict which, though it has sometimes been noted, has never been given sufficient weight.

This is quite shocking in view of its undeniability and its fatal effects on the Christian claims. Here is the conflict, and an incurable one: the *sheer logical impossibility* that God and Jesus, as defined by the Christian creeds, could have commanded and taught the hateful things the Bible says they commanded and taught, and still be loving, just, forgiving, and merciful.

Read that again; it's important.

What people understand by Hate cannot be the same as what they understand by Love. Not even God can make a square circle.

The problem here is more than the conventional question of "theodicy," the attempt to fathom a "seeming" inconsistency between God's ostensible providence on the one hand and the suffering of the world on the other. That problem revolves around the question of why God does not stop or prevent natural adversity or the crimes of humans against other humans.

By contrast, what I am talking about is the Christian, biblical belief that God or Christ has inflicted, and will inflict, horrors upon innocent humans who must thank him for it! Such a violent clash of beliefs must generate the worst cognitive dissonance migraine imaginable. The offending clash of cold and warm fronts must eventuate in a terrible storm.

Trying to split the difference by dubbing this theological train-wreck an "antinomy" or a "mystery" is the theological equivalent of a lobotomy. One must evacuate either of the beliefs of any literal, straightforward meaning, and this only reduces either tenet to gibberish. No claim is any longer being made.

Once I Was Blind, but Now I See
Reading the Bible with clear eyes

Have you ever been to the eye doctor and taken that test where the ophthalmologist covers one of your eyes with the little black plastic paddle and tests how well you can see out of your other eye? Sure you have. I find it interesting that sometimes you seem actually to see better with one eye when the other is covered. Maybe I'm wrong. Maybe I'm hallucinating. But maybe you are, too, about other things.

To me, it seems that the religious believer *thinks* he sees the world (even the invisible part of it!) quite well. He thinks he has a good grasp on the world as Christian dogma defines it. But what if this seeming clarity depends upon his not seeing through the other eye, the one artificially blinded? If he opened that eye, if he removed the plastic obstruction, things might look a lot different.

Many of us can attest that opening the covered eye, when it comes to the Bible and its difficulties, automatically throws things into a new and much sharper focus. As agonizing as you fear it will be to reappraise your faith, the rewards will be great.

Ironically, the rewards are especially rich for anyone with a keen interest in the Bible. Once you drop the notion that the Bible is an infallible revelation from God, the Bible falls into place as an altogether *human* creation. You will recognize all those stubborn "biblical difficulties" that seemed to threaten your belief in inspiration as perfectly normal features of a man-made book.

What a relief! No more telling yourself that those once-troubling verses don't really mean what they look like they mean. You can stop kidding yourself. What's more, you will experience a flood of new light on the text. Long-standing problems become clues to solve biblical puzzles. You get what you always wanted: a convincing and natural reading of your favorite book.

It seems only common sense that an approach that provides solutions to conundrums in the text is preferable to an approach that creates *obstacles* to understanding it. Give yourself the freedom to do that. I predict that you will find the study of the Bible much more fascinating and exciting than ever before, just as I have.

You may ask why you would continue to read the Bible if you gave up faith in it. Well, were you only interested in this book as a Christian because you thought you *had* to be, as one of the "course requirements" for being a Christian? That is damning the Bible with faint praise! The Bible is *inherently* fascinating. One does not need a theological justification for wanting to understand it.

OnStar of Bethlehem

A biblical criticism example

Let's start by looking at a particular example of a well-known passage: Matthew's nativity story (Matt. 2:1-23). It teems with problems that defy a reading of it as the infallible Word of God, and that make perfect sense as tell-tale signs of purely human origin.

There is a strange inconsistency in the story. At first, we are given to believe that the Magi (Zoroastrian astrologers) simply interpreted the rising of a star, presumably in the constellation of Pisces. This constellation had been assigned to Israel, as other constellations were assigned to other nations.

To them the star signaled the birth of a new heir to the throne of Judea. This is why they seek out King Herod in Jerusalem. They must assume the baby is Herod's own new son and heir, so they go to Jerusalem, expecting to find him there. Herod, of course, has no new son and so wonders if the Magi mean the prophesied Messianic king. But he doesn't know the specifics, so he calls in his scripture scholars, who do know: The Messianic king would have to be born in humble Bethlehem, just like David, whose royal dynasty the Messiah would resume.

Herod is not Davidic, not even ethnically Jewish, being instead half Idumean (Edomite), half Arab. So he is automatically suspicious: If some schemers in Bethlehem are promoting a local infant as the Messianic king, this means they are planning to act on his behalf, using the boy as a standard of revolt against the hated, faux-Jewish Herod. He tells the Magi to search for the child in Bethlehem and, when they have found him, to return and report on his whereabouts.

Herod secretly plans to send soldiers to kill the child and nip a plot against him in the bud. They locate him all right, but are commanded by an angel not to return to Herod. So they present their gifts to baby Jesus and return home (the Parthian Empire) by a different route, skipping Jerusalem. Herod discovers their treachery but determines that he will go ahead with his plan anyway, the only hitch being that, not having been given any specific address, he will have to kill every male child two years old and under to make sure he gets the right one.

In all this, the only miracle, if you can call it that, is the angelic warnings being given to the Magi. There is nothing about any strange celestial body appearing out of nowhere. Nothing about the motion of a star through the night sky like a satellite, leading them to Jerusalem. It was the astrological significance of the "regularly scheduled" motion of the stars that told the Magi that their destination must be Jerusalem.

But then, after Herod tells them to try Bethlehem, we read that the star *reappeared* (had it disappeared in the meantime?) and guided them to Bethlehem. Uh, why? Couldn't Herod's scribes (or pretty much anybody else) have given the Magi simple directions? The star goes ahead of them like a celestial GPS device, finally stopping directly over the house of Mary and Joseph, residents of Bethlehem (unlike Luke's version, where they are visitors to Bethlehem from Nazareth and have to bunk in a stable).

Of course, no star can pinpoint an individual hovel from high up in space. We are no longer talking about a star, as in the beginning of the story of the Magi. We are talking about Tinkerbell. I don't see how you're going to iron out this whopping contradiction, which would seem to be your duty as long as you want to regard the narrative as infallible and inerrant.

Does it help if you just say, "Okay, it's a bit confusing, but whatever the point is, it's inerrant"? Inerrant, but inconsistent—that's great.

Why not just *get real* and admit someone wanted to amp up the supernatural Technicolor of the story by adding the ridiculous moving "star" while failing to notice how it made a mess of the original version? At least this way the contradictions make sense *as contradictions*. You just need to drop the insistence that there can *be* no contradictions because you're reading the "Word of God."

But it gets worse, *much* worse. If we go back, as fundamentalists do, and reread the first part of the story in light of verses 9 and 10 ("And lo, the star which they had seen in the East went before them, till it came to rest over the place where the child was. When they saw the star, they rejoiced exceedingly with great joy."), we have to infer that the star was some new celestial object after all. So it was this thing and not the standard astrological chart that led the Magi, flying through the heavens above them.

But then you have to ask why the Tinkerbell star first led them to Jerusalem, *the wrong town*–and much worse–to Herod, who only became aware of the birth of a potential rival after the Magi inquired about the newborn King of the Jews. It was then and only then that Herod resolved to kill Jesus. Why didn't God's celestial homing device lead them directly to Bethlehem in the first place, as it eventually wound up doing anyway? Then Herod would have had no knowledge of the birth and no reason to dispatch a death squad to kill all the baby boys of Bethlehem!

An angel did tell them to skip Jerusalem on the way home, after all. So why not tell them to skip it and go right to Bethlehem in the first place? If the divine goal was simply to protect Jesus, then why not leave the paranoid Herod out of it altogether? Then Herod would not have known and there would never have been a slaughter of the innocents.

Does this not suggest that it was God's intention that they be slaughtered? He surely knew they would be. In fact, the Bible says it was prophesied:

> When Herod the king heard this, he was troubled, and all Jerusalem with him; and assembling all the chief priests and scribes of the people, he inquired of them where the Christ was to be born. They told him, "In Bethlehem of Judea; for so it is written by the prophet: 'And you, O Bethlehem, in the land of Judah, are by no means least among the rulers of Judah; for from you shall come a ruler who will govern my people Israel." (Matt. 2: 3-6)

Is it possible, with words meaning to us what they do, that a God who can do anything and knows everything which has ever happened or will ever happen—who is a loving, just and merciful father—would deliberately cause such an unjust and fatal miracle?

Is there no escape from the unhappy moral conclusion that God knowingly caused the slaughter of innocents?

Yes, there *is* a way: You can relinquish the arbitrary belief that God inspired the writing of this text and that therefore it must be historically accurate. Then it becomes all too clear that God was arranging nothing, but that "Matthew" the evangelist (gospel writer) was.

And his goal? It was a purely literary one: He wanted to create a Christian version of the nativity story of Moses as it was being (re)told at the time.

We read in Josephus' *Antiquities of the Jews* how Pharaoh, learning from his own scribes that a Hebrew child should soon be born who would bring Egypt to her knees and deliver the Hebrew slaves, ordered that all male Hebrew babies were to be killed, just to make sure they got the right one. Baby Moses was providentially delivered from the tyrant's persecution, though the rest of the Hebrew boys were not so lucky! But the Exodus writer was not really concerned with them. They were just "extras" on the stage of the play he was writing. It never happened: No Jewish baby boys were slaughtered. In exactly the same way, the Bethlehem innocents meant nothing to Matthew. They were just stage props, like wax fruit on the kitchen table on stage.

Once, when I served as a pastor, my eyes widened as the children's choir sang a jaunty little number about Noah's Flood. When the waters receded, God placed the rainbow in the sky as a mark of his faithfulness. As the song title said, it was God's "rainbow valentine" to the human race (or what was left of it!).

I shouldn't have, but I stepped up to the pulpit and quipped that a better title might have been "Rainbow Epitaph." There was nothing in the lyrics about the horrible death of the fledgling human race, outside of Noah and his family. But of course the writer of the silly song wasn't taking it seriously as history, right? The soggy, bloated corpses that must have littered the ground were not real people. They were, again, window dressing. So who cares what happened to them, since nothing really did!

You could, I suppose, just skip the difficulty-laden Matthew and turn to Luke's nativity instead, as people usually do on Christmas Eve, since baby massacres are kind of a downer on such a charming occasion. But will that really solve the problem? Both nativities are divinely inspired, aren't they? Read them side by side (which I'm betting you've never done) and you will quickly see how glaringly different they are from one another at virtually every point.

In Luke, it is shepherds tending their flocks who are told by an angel that they will find Jesus lying in a manger–not Mary and Joseph's home. And that is where they found him, without any star of Bethlehem. Nor was there any Herod, or, best of all, any slaughter of every innocent male baby in and around Bethlehem!

Is it not strange that the *divinely inspired* versions of Matthew and Luke should be so diametrically different? The very need to choose which story is the true one is all the proof needed that the Bible was entirely man-made–which explains why it is riddled by absurdities, historical errors and outright contradictions such as these.

A Literary Solution?
Humane recognition of a human Bible

The man-made character of the Bible also fully explains the greatest contradiction and impossibility of all: that a loving, just and merciful father will consign most of humanity to eternal punishment. For, as I will discuss in a later chapter, the tender babe of Bethlehem will grow up to issue blood-chilling declamations like this one:

> Enter ye in at the narrow gate: for wide is the gate, and broad is the way that leadeth to destruction, and many there are who go in thereat. How narrow is the gate, and strait is the way that leadeth to life: and few there are that find it! (Matt. 7:13-14, KJV)

Think of it: just two groups, many sent to eternal suffering and only a few to salvation—the arithmetic of hell!

Facing the truth about the Bible and its God will not, as you have probably been bullied into believing, smash morality, undermining any and all standards of right and wrong. It will not require the slightest adjustment to the meaning of words like "love," "justice," "forgiveness," and "mercy" as they are instinctively understood by all civilized people everywhere. Goodness remains unscathed, and Truth will out.

Notes

1. *Inerrant the Wind*, a slightly updated reprint of the dissertation in book form, is available from Prometheus Books (2009).

2. Declaration "Dominus Iesus" on the Unicity and Salvific Universality of Jesus Christ and the Church, Introduction. Congregation for the Doctrine of the Faith, vatican.va [vatican.va/roman_curia/congregations/cfaith/documents/rc_con_cfaith_doc_20000806_dominus-iesus_en.html].

I

The Son Who Is the Father

> If God wrote the Old Testament and afterward came upon the
> earth as Jesus Christ, and taught a new religion, and the Jews
> crucified him, was this not in accordance with his own law, and
> was he not, after all, the victim of himself?

> —Robert G. Ingersoll,
> interviewed in *The Chicago Times*, May 29, 1881.

One and One and One Is Three

He's gotta be good-looking 'cause he's so hard to see

In Matthew 22:42, Jesus poses the question, "What do you think of
the Christ? Whose son is he?" Good question, no? If Jesus was the
Son, who was the Father? God, naturally. Jesus referred to him
often.

He is, of course, a monotheist. When asked to rank the
commandments, Jesus replies, "The first is, 'Hear O Israel: The
Lord our God, the Lord is one'" (Mark 12:29). And "this is eternal
life, that they know thee, the only true God" (John 17:3).

Jesus often refers to God simply as "the Father," but that doesn't
really explain Jesus' own relation to God. Likewise, many times he
teaches about "*your* Father in heaven," but the topic there is *his
followers'* relation to God. Here are a number of the passages in
which Jesus speaks of his *own* relation to "*my* Father who is in
heaven."

Matthew 7:21

When he warns that "Not every one who says to me, 'Lord, Lord,'
shall enter the kingdom of heaven, but he who does the will of my
Father who is in heaven," Jesus is certainly stressing that mere
words will not guarantee salvation; true righteousness is required.
But there is another, implicit, point to be considered: the integral
connection between his own lordly authority and that of his Father.

To be able to claim rightly that Jesus is your Lord, i.e., that you obey his orders, is tantamount to obeying the commands (the will) of his Father. Ultimately these two authorities are one and the same.

Matthew 10:32-33

Whoever "acknowledges me before men, I also will acknowledge before my Father who is in heaven; but whoever denies me before men, I also will deny before my Father who is in heaven." Here the scene Jesus envisions is that of the Final Judgment. Though, as we have just observed, mere lip service to Jesus' lordship is worthless, one might say it is a necessary first step. You might confess allegiance to Jesus and belie it with your actions, but if you do not even get *that* far, you cannot expect that, on the Last Day, Jesus is going to put in a good word for you with his Father.

God is going to want to know if you took a stand for Jesus. Only after that will he ask if your deeds made a mockery of your profession. But *no* profession?

Matthew 11:27

Jesus' own exalted status in this world and the next is based on his relation to God as a son to a father, as a prince to a king. "All things have been delivered to me by my Father; and no one knows the Son except the Father, and no one knows the Father except the Son and anyone to whom the Son chooses to reveal him." How is Jesus even in a position to reveal the truth about God, unlike the rest of us who can only guess? He knows all about God because he has intimate, *familial* knowledge, "a chip off the old block."

Matthew 16

After Peter has successfully done what Jesus has required us to do if we wish him to give us the thumbs-up at the Final Judgment, namely confess him before others, Jesus congratulates him. "Flesh and blood has not revealed this to you, but my Father who is in heaven" (v. 17). Peter has uttered his conviction that Jesus is the Son of the living God, the kind of thing no one could know without supernatural information from God himself.

By saying this, Jesus signals that he knows both the facts of his own sonship and that that can be known to another only by revelation. How can Jesus know such things? He does not need the Father to reveal it to *him*. No, he is already "in the loop." He comes from the place (the "other side") where revelations come from. Unlike Peter (or Moses, for that matter–see John 1:17-18), Jesus is naturally at home there.

Matthew 18

Another example of Jesus' "inside information" concerning his divine Father and his celestial realm meets us in Matthew 18:11: "See that you do not despise one of these little ones; for I tell you that in heaven their angels always behold the face of my Father who is in heaven." How does he know this? He has been there, in the immediate presence of his Father and his attendant angels.

In verse 19, he says, "If two of you agree on earth about anything they ask, it will be done for them by my Father in heaven." Again, this is not presented as some surmise by a theologian, but as information from someone directly acquainted with God's "policies" toward mortals. It is like a government official explaining to students how the government operates. He knows from experience.

In verses 34-35, Jesus concludes a long parable about God's forgiveness being conditional upon our forgiving one another with this chilling warning: "And in anger his lord delivered him to the torturers, till he should pay all his debt. So also my heavenly Father will do to every one of you, if you do not forgive your brother from your heart." Yikes! But better to know than not to!

John

Who would presume to speak in such a way for almighty God? Someone on the inside, someone who sits at the right hand of God, that's who. And the same is true for several more of Jesus' sayings about the God he calls "my Father." These are all from John, the gospel with the most "high Christology," i.e., the loftiest view of Jesus as more than a mere mortal.

- "You shall not make my Father's house a house of trade" (John 2:16).

- "My Father is working still, and I am working" (John 5:17).

- "My Father gives you the true bread from heaven" (John 6:32).

- "This is the will of my Father, that every one who sees the Son and believes in him should have eternal life" (John 6:40).

- "The works that I do in my Father's name, they bear witness to me" (John 10:25).

- "My Father, who has given them to me, is greater than all" (John 10:29).

- "If I am not doing the works of my Father, then do not believe me" (John 10:37).

The implicit claim underlying all of them can be summed up neatly in this one: "I speak of what I have seen with my Father" (John 8:38).

Again, who is his Father? Jesus is plainly referring to the deity of the Old Testament, Yahweh (or, perhaps more familiarly, "Jehovah"): the Creator, he who issued the Ten Commandments to Moses (John 5:46), he who sent Isaiah (John 12:37-41). This is especially clear in John 8:54: "It is my Father who glorifies me, of whom you say that he is your God."

But it goes much farther than that. Jesus actually identifies himself with, or even *as*, the heavenly Father!

"I proceeded and came forth from God" he says in John 8:42. One might understand this passage as a more modest claim that Jesus was sent on his mission like any of the Old Testament prophets. Isaiah, Jeremiah, Amos, and the rest could have properly used the same words. But, given other things Jesus says in John, I translate it as a much stronger claim: "I proceeded and emerged from the Godhead."

For many readers, John 8:58, "Before Abraham was, I am," would seem to be a forthright claim by Jesus to be Jehovah: "I am who I am. Tell the people of Israel, 'I Am has sent me to you'" (Exod. 3:14). But I fear this is a mistranslation.[2] It should be rendered simply as "I existed before Abraham," which is still a pretty exalted claim of divine pre-existence.

"I and the Father are one" is his claim in John 10:30. I think that's pretty clear. Some would start back-pedaling at this point, as if all Jesus meant was, "I and my Father are always in agreement," but that sounds like an attempt to water down the text by some who would prefer to view Jesus merely as a prophet.

An even stronger assertion of his divinity occurs in John 14:9, "He who has seen me has seen the Father."[3] I see the same point being made in John 8:19: "You know neither me nor my Father; if you knew me you would know my Father also" (John 8:19).

Finally, there is the Doubting Thomas episode in John 20. Convinced that Jesus has truly risen from the dead, Thomas bows before him and exclaims, "My Lord and my God!" (v. 28). He is not just uttering, "My God!", as we sometimes do when something takes us by surprise. The Greek text puts Thomas' confession in the vocative case, meaning he is speaking directly to Jesus.

Trinity Training Wheels

I want to emphasize an important point. You will notice that Jesus both identifies his Father with Jehovah, the Old Testament God, *and* that he identifies himself with his Father, Jehovah. This is where we get the Trinity.

The familiar word "Trinity" is a contraction for "tri-unity," i.e., "three-in-one." The doctrine of the Trinity stipulates that the Father, the Son, and the Holy Spirit (or "Holy Ghost") are three distinct persons (centers of consciousness), sharing a single divine nature.

If we say that Dick, Jane, and Sally are three persons sharing a single *human* nature, all we mean is that Dick, Jane, and Sally are three members of the same category: They are three human beings. This makes them a *trio*, but not a *trinity*. So why are Father, Son, and Holy Spirit more than a trio of gods, like Zeus, Hera, and Apollo? Theologians have speculated that in the case of the Christian God, the "nature" that the three share is somehow more "real," more "substantial," than the "nature" shared by all created things (whatever that might mean).

The doctrine of the Trinity is so important to Christian belief that the relatively few sects who reject it, yet still consider themselves Christian, are denied the name by everyone else. For instance, the Church of Jesus Christ of Latter-day Saints (Mormons for short) are not Trinitarians. They are technically *polytheists* since they understand the Father and the Son as two distinct beings, each with humanoid physical bodies. The Holy Spirit is, of course, a disembodied entity.

The Worldwide Church of God (once known as the Radio Church of God and now as Grace Communion International) is *Binitarian*, accepting the essential unity of Father and Son, who are persons, but regarding the Spirit as more of an impersonal force. Christadelphians are *Adoptionists*, believing that Jesus Christ was not the incarnation of a heavenly being, but rather a supremely righteous man whom God rewarded by exalting him to the place of honor at his right hand (his "right-hand man," as we say). His "sonship" is an honorific title.

Jehovah's Witnesses are *Arians*, espousing the ancient doctrines of Arius, believing that Jesus Christ was not God in the flesh, but rather the incarnation of an exalted but created being, the Word (*Logos*) of God. This doctrine is based on their reading of the somewhat ambiguous John 1:1, "In the beginning was the Word, and the Word was with God, and the Word was *theos*." How should we translate the word *theos*? It is the same word translated elsewhere in the same verse as "God," but in this particular instance there is no article before the noun.

In Greek, if you intend to refer to a particular thing, even a proper name, you introduce it with a definite article, "the," even if you wouldn't, for the sake of style, retain it in English translation. In English, of course, we also use the indefinite article, "a" or "an," if we don't have a specific thing or person in mind ("an American," "a patriot"). In Greek, though, there *is* no indefinite article; you just leave out any article. In John 1:1, "God" is preceded by "the" the first and second times, so we know the reference is to "God." But the third time there is no article before *theos*.

The ancient Arians thought, as do today's Jehovah's Witnesses, that we ought to render the last part of John 1:1 as "and the Word was a god." That may indeed have been what the author meant to say, and it's a good translation. But it's not the only possibility. In most Bibles you will instead find "and the Word was God." Why? Because of another Greek grammar rule. *Theos* is not a direct object here, as if you said, "I love God." It is a predicate nominative, as in "Julian is the man!" Well, in a case like that, for some reason, in Greek you could skip the definite article even if you did intend a particular *theos*. Thus, we're back at square one. It could just as easily mean "The Word was (the) God."

You might prefer one of these understandings to one that seems to make nonsense of simple arithmetic, decreeing that three can simultaneously be one, and that one can be the same as three. But we must remember a crucial point: Those early bishops who formulated the doctrine after much serious scriptural and philosophical debate never pretended that it "made sense," that they were "explaining" anything. No, they admitted forthrightly that the Trinity was forever a mystery that mere human minds could never fathom.

Given the notion of an infinite and eternal deity, should it be any surprise that we have only glimpses of him? As Job said, "Lo, these are but the outskirts of his ways; and how small a whisper do we hear of him!" (Job 26:14). God appears to Job, who had been claiming God was treating him unfairly, and rebuked him for his presumption. To paraphrase, he says to the terrified Job, "You can't even begin to explain the phenomena of nature! How the birds know to migrate, what arranges the stars in their constellations. And you think you can understand *me* well enough to hold me to account?" Still a good point!

As twentieth-century theologian Karl Barth warned, any "God" that we, with our worm's eye-view, could neatly comprehend would automatically have to be an idol, a fiction, a figment of the speculative imagination. What the old fourth-century theologians were trying to do was to set some boundary markers, to rule out *over-simplifications*. They were trying to say, in effect, what the Trinity was *not*.

So it might actually be less misleading to speak of the *mystery* of the Trinity than of the *doctrine* of the Trinity. (Some theologians do exactly that.) "Doctrines" of the Trinity would *ipso facto* be wrong-headed oversimplifications. That is why Mormons, Jehovah's Witnesses, Christadelphians, etc., are so widely written off by Catholics, Protestants, and Eastern Orthodox as heretics.

The Athanasian Creed, mistakenly ascribed to Athanasius of Alexandria, was composed somewhere in the late fifth or early sixth centuries by the churchman Vincent of Lerins in Southern Gaul. It provides the classic definition of Trinitarianism:

> WE worship one God in Trinity, and Trinity in Unity;
>
> NEITHER confounding the persons nor dividing the substance.
>
> FOR there is one person of the Father, another of the Son, and another of the Holy Spirit.
>
> BUT the Godhead of the Father, of the Son, and of the Holy Spirit is all one, the glory equal, the majesty coeternal.
>
> SUCH as the Father is, such is the Son, and such is the Holy Spirit.
>
> THE Father uncreated, the Son uncreated, and the Holy Spirit uncreated.

THE Father incomprehensible, the Son incomprehensible, and the Holy Spirit incomprehensible.

THE Father eternal, the Son eternal, and the Holy Spirit eternal.

AND yet they are not three eternals but one eternal.

As also there are not three uncreated nor three incomprehensible, but one uncreated and one incomprehensible.

So likewise the Father is almighty, the Son almighty, and the Holy Spirit almighty.

AND yet they are not three almighties, but one almighty.

So the Father is God, the Son is God, and the Holy Spirit is God;

AND yet they are not three Gods, but one God.

So likewise the Father is Lord, the Son Lord, and the Holy Spirit Lord;

AND yet they are not three Lords but one Lord.

FOR like as we are compelled by the Christian verity to acknowledge every Person by himself to be God and Lord;

So are we forbidden by the catholic religion to say; There are three Gods or three Lords.

THE Father is made of none, neither created nor begotten.

THE Son is of the Father alone; not made nor created, but begotten.

THE Holy Spirit is of the Father and of the Son; neither made, nor created, nor begotten, but proceeding.

So there is one Father, not three Fathers; one Son, not three Sons; one Holy Spirit, not three Holy Spirits.

AND in this Trinity none is afore or after another; none is greater or less than another.

BUT the whole three persons are coeternal, and coequal.

So that in all things, as aforesaid, the Unity in Trinity and the Trinity in Unity is to be worshipped.

HE therefore that will be saved must thus think of the Trinity.[1]

Just one more word about Trinity and heresy. You may be a heretic and not even know it! Have you ever "explained" the Trinity with the (supposed) analogy of water? Water is H_2O, but we find it in three very different forms: liquid water, solid ice, and gaseous steam. It changes back and forth as the temperature rises and falls. Just like the Trinity, right? Same underlying substance but three different modes of being or activity depending on God's purposes at any given time. Uh, if that's what you think, my friend, then you are indeed a heretic, because that analogy does not fit Trinitarianism. No, you are talking *Modalism*, the belief that Father, Son, and Spirit are *external* to the Godhead, three ways in which the one God appears.

Do you prefer the analogy that God is like one man who embraces the very different roles of a husband, a father, and, say, an insurance salesman? Modalism again, I'm afraid. It's one guy who's doing three sets of things. Trinitarianism, by contrast, envisions "threeness" as *internal* to God.

Or maybe you have heard someone try illustrating the Trinity as three light bulbs wired in series, like your Christmas tree lights. You turn them on, and they contribute to a common illumination. See? Three bulbs are giving out a single blaze of light. Only that would be *Tritheism*, the belief in three distinct deities. Now you might think this is better than baffling Trinitarianism, but you have to admit that it *isn't* Trinitarianism.

It is important that, even if we cannot actually fathom what the Trinity *is*, we get straight what it is *not*, if we are to be able to search out its true implications.

The Trinity in the Bible

I have noted that Trinitarianism was hammered out as late as the fourth century by bishop-theologians, bringing both philosophical and biblical tools into play. This does not mean the Trinity was an *ad hoc* invention. They understood themselves to be gathering and systematizing the relevant data of scripture. It was never simply a matter of mere proof-texting, heedless of context. To have approached the question the way they did implies that they knew that the Bible did not simply "teach the Trinity" as many naïve believers seem today to suppose.

I don't want to be misunderstood here: I am not saying that only the naïve embrace Trinitarianism. I just mean that, when they claim it is a biblical teaching, they are over-simplifying the matter, telescoping something complex.

The Trinity emerged from a deep and difficult process. The Bible contains no statement like the one just quoted from the Athanasian Creed. Another great theologian and philosopher, Paul Tillich,[4] observed that the Bible does not speak in philosophical terms, but it does raise questions that invite, even demand, philosophical answers. That, I think, is the way we ought to understand the Christian position on the Trinity.

So what New Testament data are we talking about here? References to "Lord Jesus Christ, God, and the Holy Spirit" (2 Cor. 13:14) are of no help, since they contain no hint as to how the three are supposed to be related. As Arthur W. Wainwright[5] says in his excellent book, *The Trinity in the New Testament*, the doctrine of the Trinity stems from certain self-declarations of Jesus in the Gospel of John.

- "I proceeded and came forth from God" (John 8:42)
- "I existed before Abraham." (John 8:58)
- "I and the Father are one" (John 10: 30)

- "He who has seen me has seen the Father." (John 14:9)

- "My Lord and my God!" (John 20:28).

So, you see, Jesus and Jehovah are *one and the same God*. I want to make you see some pretty surprising implications that are often, even usually, missed. Perhaps Bible-readers *have* sensed them but repressed them. You'll see why as we proceed.

Notes

1. "Athanasian Creed," Christian Classics Ethereal Library, ccel.org/creeds/athanasian.creed.html.

2. Jason David BeDuhn, *Truth in Translation: Accuracy and Bias in English Translations of the New Testament* (Lanham, MD: University Press of America, 2003), pp. 103-107.

3. Verse 11, "Or do you not believe that I am in the Father and the Father in me," also reeks of scribal retreat from too bold-seeming a declaration.

4. Paul Tillich, *Biblical Religion and the Search for Ultimate Reality.* James W. Richard Lectures in the Christian Religion (Chicago: University of Chicago Press, 1955), pp. 82-85.

5. Arthur W. Wainwright, *The Trinity in the New Testament* (London: SPCK, 1969), pp. 250, 260-266.

II

Artists' Conceptions of Jesus

> Jesus! thou art all compassion,
> Pure, unbounded love thou art...

—Charles Wesley

What do Christians have in mind when they strive to be "Christlike"? When they ponder the question "What would Jesus do?" What sort of individual do evangelical Christians picture when they imagine a "personal relationship with Jesus"? What do liberal Christians mean when they say "the personality of Jesus" is the essence of Christianity?

I think it is safe to say they have all cobbled together various appealing and admirable traits associated with the Jesus character they read about in the gospels. As we will see, it's a pretty selective portrait.

Whosoever Will May Come

I have always been struck with the approachability of Jesus in the gospel stories. No matter how long the day, no matter how great the need, Jesus is shown welcoming anyone who seeks him out. No one is unimportant to him, no one unworthy of his time.

It shows both a respect for "the least of [his] brethren" (Matt. 25:40) and a heartfelt compassion for them, like a father for his children. In Matthew 8:2-3, a leper approaches him, asking to be healed. Despite the fact that skin disease sufferers would transmit ritual uncleanness to any who touched them, Jesus does not hesitate, unlike the self-absorbed, high-and-mighty priest and Levite who stepped over the broken form of a mugging victim on the roadside so as not to ruin their ceremonial "sterility" for the upcoming Temple service (Luke 10:31-32).

Likewise, in Matthew 8:5-7, a Roman centurion approaches Jesus to ask a favor which would entail Jesus crossing the cultural boundary between pious Jews and pagan Romans. He wants him to heal his servant. Jesus does not hesitate to respond to the need of a member of the military force occupying his country. Some would no doubt have thought Jesus should ignore him, that helping him would constitute aiding and abetting the enemy. But Jesus' first allegiance is to those in need, whatever their nationality or their politics.

Matthew 9:20-22 shows Jesus–like Dr. Marcus Welby, medical bag in hand–on his way to one sick patient when he is accosted by an old lady determined to draw off a bit of his healing aura. He takes time for her, patiently hears the woman out, blesses her for her faith, then goes his way.

Some parents want Jesus to hold their babies and utter some blessing over them, as if to grant them a healthy, prosperous future (Matt. 19:13-15). His disciples, who are unwittingly projecting their own inflated sense of self-importance onto their Master, shoo them away. "Jesus is too busy to waste his precious time with children!" they say.

But he doesn't agree. He shoos his *disciples* away, welcoming the infants as honored guests–ambassadors of the kingdom of heaven! He sees value in human beings in whom others see only a nuisance. There is no one for whom he does not have time.

A Compassionate Christ

When Jesus beholds a swelling sea of the afflicted lining up to see him, his automatic reaction is compassion. He has pity for the clueless, aimless sheep looking to him, hoping they have found their good shepherd at last (Matt. 9:36-38).

In Matthew 14:13-14, Jesus has sought out a momentary retreat from his ministry of healing, only to find that his movements have nonetheless been discovered. Yet another desperately needy multitude is waiting for him. They have no thought that Jesus, too, gets tired and needs rest. Their own pains and plights blind them to all else. Is Jesus stung with resentment? No, compassion renews his strength. Selflessness enables him to see only their needs, not his own.

What moves Jesus to multiply the loaves and fishes for a hungry crowd (Matt. 15:32)? Is he trying to prove something? Trying to vindicate his claims to divine authority? Nothing of the sort! He is afraid these dear people will faint from hunger. And they never even know he did a miracle for them.

In Luke 7:13, Jesus happens upon a funeral. An old widow weeps for her son who has been for years her only pillar of support. Jesus does what all mourners wish they could do: He raises the dead man. He displays the power of compassion. Compassion could not enable us to do what Jesus did, but the story bids us do what we can.

Friend of Sinners

The compassion of Jesus for his fellow men is nowhere more evident than in his non-judgmental dealings with "sinners." Those were Jews deemed social outcasts because of their links to the Roman administration (e.g., tax-collectors, Luke 19:1-10), prostitutes (Luke 7:36-50), and people who generally cared little for the restrictions of the Jewish Law ("Sorry, rabbi, but I'm not religious.").

I say "non-judgmental," but in the particular sense that he seems to have put his cards on the table while still wanting to play the game. Unlike some of the pious who simply avoided the sinners for fear of being corrupted by association with them (1 Cor. 15:33), Jesus leaves no doubt that he hates the sin, as if to say, "Look, you know, and I know, that you need to repent." But, as the cliché goes, he loves the sinner, as the parable of the Prodigal Son (Luke 15:11-32) makes clear.

No matter how deep in debt you are (a striking and traditional metaphor for one's "rap sheet" with God), God's (and Jesus') only priority is to get you cleaned up and back in the fold. That's the whole point of the Lost Sheep parable in Luke 15:1-7.

Thus Jesus' policy, quite controversial to some, of seeking out sinners and telling them of God's offered amnesty. In Mark 2:14-17 he uses irresistible common sense to defend his practice of associating with sinners: "Those who are well have no need for a physician, but those who are sick. I came to call not the righteous, but sinners." If the righteous are the salt of the earth whose job is to preserve and to flavor it (Matt. 5:13), they will do no good by remaining in the shaker.

John 7:53-8:11 gives us the most striking case of Jesus' love for sinners and his willingness, not to abolish moral standards, but to give sinners a second chance and to urge them to take it. A pious mob, seething with indignation (rather like the morality-enforcement vigilante squads in Saudi Arabia), wants Jesus' endorsement of their plan to execute an adulteress. There could be no doubt of her guilt; she had been caught in the act, one supposes by her husband (as also happens in the semi-comedic Proverbs chapter seven). Where is the adulterer? My guess is that he had been dealt with already, also by the cuckolded husband!

Well, Jesus says he has no problem with it—as long as the eager would-be executioners are quite sure they have the moral superiority to act as her judges. The thought is not that no human being has the right to execute another. No, the point is to say that they don't *have* to press charges this particular time. Haven't they committed serious sins of their own at one time or another? Wouldn't you, or didn't you, appreciate it when someone let *you* off with a warning? Why not give this woman a break?

There is a very important point here, to which we shall return in another connection: What good will deadly punishment do? It brings no increase of righteousness, that's for sure. On the other hand, mercy leading to repentance does. Everybody's a winner. Keep that in mind.

Love and Forgiveness

Many in our day would likely sum up the teaching of Jesus in one word: "love." There are several powerful New Testament texts about love (e.g., 1 John 4:20-21: "If anyone says, 'I love God,' and hates his brother, he is a liar; for he who does not love his brother whom he has seen, how can he love God whom he has not seen?"). Though there is a surprising paucity of such statements quoted from Jesus himself in the gospels, all you really need is John 13:34:

> A new commandment I give to you, that you love one another; even as I have loved you, that you also love one another. By this all men will know that you are my disciples, if you have love for one another.

A key aspect of love is, of course, forgiveness. The lack of it—or should we say, the *refusal* of it—is a wall that love cannot penetrate. The one who loves is one who forgives. The one who refuses to forgive ceases to love. Paul says, "Love never fails" (1 Cor. 13:8), which means that, if it is real, it never peters out.

Jesus' way of saying the same thing is on display in Matthew 18:21-22: "Then Peter came up and said to him, 'Lord, how often shall my brother sin against me, and I forgive him? As many as seven times?' Jesus said to him, 'I do not say to you seven times, but seventy times seven.'" Obviously, it doesn't have to be very many times before you confront your brother and try to get to the bottom of the problem. You try to prevent recurrence of the offense. But that's what you do; you don't repudiate him: "You're dead to me, Andrew!"

Nursing a grudge befouls and stifles the sense of devotion and piety. "If you forgive men their trespasses, your heavenly Father also will forgive you; but if you do not forgive men their trespasses, neither will your Father forgive your trespasses" (Matt. 6:14-15). In other words, we know instinctively that the bitterness we harbor is poisonous to the grateful heart that reverences God.

Did Jesus merely mouth the slogans of love and forgiveness? Talk is cheap, action is not. And the Jesus we meet in the pages of the gospels lived up to his words. As he faced the immediate prospect of death, he reminded the disciples of the love he would soon enact on their behalf: "Greater love has no man than this, that a man lay down his life for his friends" (John 15:13). Accordingly, Jesus forgives even the most grievous offenses, from both his enemies and his friends.

On the cross itself, far from railing against those who put him there and relishing the prospect of divine vengeance upon them, Jesus pities them: "Father, forgive them, for they know not what they do" (Luke 23:34). Once he is resurrected, he confronts Peter who, having denied him in order to save his miserable hide, dares not look him in the face (or so I must imagine it). But instead of dressing him down, Jesus offers him forgiveness and reinstates him.

Ability and Humility

What is humility? I should say it amounts to realistic self-assessment, admitting one's gifts, but being grateful for them instead of patting oneself on the back for them (1 Cor. 4:7, "What have you that you did not receive?"). The humble person, when congratulated for some talent, replies, "Yes, I'm lucky that way."

Humility also entails the maturity to laugh at pretentiousness and pomposity as the marks of a fool, especially in one's own case. It has nothing to do with false modesty or self-deprecation, which are, after all, passive-aggressive ways of boasting. To hear some people talk, you'd think Jesus had told them, "I will make you fishers for compliments."

Adults have learned that they must adopt poses to get ahead in the world. If they do not deserve respect, they have learned to assert their authority in order to *compel* respect. The more important they think they are, the more they will remind others of that "fact." But children are unpretentious. They play innocent games (Matt. 11:16-

17) and have not yet learned to play the games of over-compensation and intimidation. That is why Jesus warns, "Whoever humbles himself like this child, he is the greatest in the kingdom of heaven" (Matt. 18:4). Those who do engage in pompous role-play, Jesus excoriates without mercy (Matt. 6:2, 5, 16; 23: 5-7), puncturing their pretty balloons.

Power, famously, corrupts, lending the powerful an inflated sense of self-importance, from which come license and abuse. Jesus warns his lieutenants and successors not to fall into that trap: "You know that the rulers of the Gentiles lord it over them, and their great men exercise authority over them. It shall not be so among you; but whoever would be great among you must be your servant, and whoever would be first among you must be your slave" (Matt. 20:25-27).

Likewise, "Neither be called masters, for you have one master, the Christ. He who is greatest among you shall be your servant; whoever exalts himself will be humbled, and whoever humbles himself will be exalted" (Matt. 23:11-12). How does that work? The competent one need not brag; his work speaks for itself ("Let another praise you, and not your own mouth; a stranger, and not your own lips," Prov. 27:2). But the braggart invites scrutiny that he cannot withstand.

Was Jesus humble? It sure looks that way, at least in Mark's early, low-Christology gospel. When an admirer approaches him asking, "Good teacher, what must I do to inherit eternal life?" Jesus recoils as if stung! "Why do you call me good? No one is good but God alone" (Mark 10:17-18). Never mind the implications for theology; that's not the point. The point is that Jesus (the Markan Jesus, that is) will not countenance flattery. Especially not in this case, because here he thinks if he accepted the man's praise, or even lets it pass in silence, he would be making God share his glory with another.

Servant of All

Does Jesus exemplify the virtue of serving others? Indeed he does. Pointing to his habitual refusal of privilege, he says, "The son of man also came not to be served but to serve" (Mark 10:45). Again, "Which is the greater, one who sits at table, or one who serves? Is it not the one who sits at table? But I am among you as one who serves" (Luke 22:27).

John's depiction of Jesus is no different. John 13:3-5 has Jesus flesh out his words about serving others at the Last Supper, lest any confusion remain as to how literally we are to take them:

> Jesus, knowing that the Father had given all things into his hands, and that he had come from God and was going to God, rose from supper, laid aside his garments, and girded himself with a towel. Then he poured water into a basin, and began to wash the disciples' feet, and to wipe them with the towel with which he was girded.

I'd say that's putting his money where his mouth is.

Simply This

Jesus shows a tendency towards "cutting through spiritual materialism,"[1] an impatience with the ceremonial minutiae and entangling red tape of conventional religion. With some study, you can appreciate what motivated such legalistic arabesque and filigree and how it evolved over time. And if you believe God gave the commandments, you must strive to get them right, and with as much exactitude as possible.

Fine. But, faced with the edifice of laws and rules thus built up slowly over centuries, new generations find themselves baffled and discouraged. Jesus recognizes this fact, as well as the irony that such efforts to promote religious observance wind up discouraging it, as people throw up their hands and walk away, becoming the "sinners" to whom he reaches out with a fresh vision:

> The scribes and the Pharisees sit on Moses' seat; so practice
> and observe whatever they tell you, but not what they do;
> for they preach but do not practice. They bind heavy
> burdens, hard to bear, and lay them on men's shoulders; but
> they themselves will not move them with their finger. (Matt.
> 23:2-4)

So when it comes to prayer, Jesus cuts to the chase. In Matthew
6:7-8, he takes the scalpel of common sense to the tradition of
verbose and ornate prayer: "And in praying do not heap up empty
phrases as the Gentiles do; for they think that they will be heard for
their many words. Do not be like them, for your Father knows what
you need before you ask him. Pray then like this," he says:

Our Father who art in heaven,
    Hallowed be thy name.

Thy kingdom come,
    Thy will be done,
    On earth as it is in heaven.

Give us this day our daily bread;
    And forgive us our debts,
    As we also have forgiven our debtors;
    And lead us not into temptation,
    But deliver us from evil.

That ought to do it, short and sweet. What more do you need?

In Matthew 15:10-11, Jesus even throws ritual purity (kosher)
laws into question, apparently minimizing them in favor of moral
purity:

> And he called the people to him and said to them, "Hear and
> understand: not what goes into the mouth defiles a man,
> but what comes out of the mouth, this defiles a man.

The disciples tell him the Pharisees took exception to this and ask
for an explanation. He replies:

Are you also still without understanding? Do you not see that whatever goes into the mouth passes into the stomach, and so passes on? But what comes out of the mouth proceeds from the heart, and this defiles a man. For out of the heart come evil thoughts, murder, adultery, fornication, theft, false witness, slander. These are what defile a man; but to eat with unwashed hands does not defile a man. (Matt. 15:16-20)

In Matthew 22:35-40, Jesus boils down the whole thing to just two critical commandments:

And one of them, a lawyer, asked him a question, to test him. "Teacher, which is the great commandment in the law?" And he said to him, "You shall love the Lord your God with all your heart, and with all your soul, and with all your mind." This is the great and first commandment. And a second is like it, "You shall love your neighbor as yourself." On these two commandments depend all the law and the prophets."

That is to say, what really is the *center of gravity* of the Mosaic Law? Here's what counts. Jesus was not the only one to share this view, nor does such a defining of priorities imply doing away with all the details.

But it is a step toward simplification, like a YOU ARE HERE sign amid a labyrinthine department store. Jesus warns against the danger of losing focus when he says,

Woe to you, scribes and Pharisees, hypocrites! For you tithe mint and dill and cummin, and have neglected the weightier matters of the law, justice and mercy and faith; these you ought to have done, without neglecting the others. You blind guides, straining out a gnat and swallowing a camel! (Matt. 23:23-24)

The same thing comes up in Mark 7:9-13. Jesus gets indignant about certain Jewish traditions, such as "Corban," a provision whereby an over-zealous person could donate to the Temple treasury some funds he would ordinarily have kept for the support of his parents in their declining years. Think of today's TV evangelists convincing their viewers to give them their savings rather than bequeathing the money to their children.

> And he said to them, "You have a fine way of rejecting the commandment of God, in order to keep your tradition! For Moses said, 'Honor your father and your mother'; and, 'He who speaks evil of father or mother, let him surely die'; but you say, if a man tells his father or his mother, 'What you would have gained from me is Corban' (that is, given to God)–then you no longer permit him to do anything for his father or mother, thus making void the word of God through your tradition which you hand on."

What an irony! The tradition of the scribes was meant to elucidate and to apply the commandments but winds up in effect nullifying them! Better to simplify things and clean out the rank growth.

And then there is the question of where faithful Israelites should worship. The Jerusalem Temple on Mount Zion? Or the ruins of the Samaritan Temple on Mount Gerizim?

It's moot, a distraction, says Jesus in John 4:21-24. "Jesus said to her, 'Woman, believe me, the hour is coming when neither on this mountain nor in Jerusalem will you worship the Father . . . . But the hour is coming, and now is, when the true worshipers will worship the Father in spirit and truth, for such the Father seeks to worship him. God is spirit, and those who worship him must worship in spirit and truth.'"

Holy ground is wherever you are, because wherever you are, God is, ready to listen.

Holiness and Humanism

Jesus pushed religion in the direction of common sense and ethics, away from the merely ritual. One crucial aspect of that change in emphasis was a trend toward *humanism*.

In Mark 2:27, he defends allowing his disciples to glean grain on the Sabbath. Strictly speaking, they should have planned ahead and gathered enough grain ahead of time, before the Sabbath began, avoiding the necessity to work on the Sabbath.

Sure, that's one of the commandments, but just try convincing your growling stomach that it makes any difference! God's not going to be harmed if someone picks some grain on the Sabbath, but hungry mortals may be! And it is humans' interests that Jesus wants protected: "The Sabbath was made for man, not man for the Sabbath" (Mark 2:27).

Courage and Character

No one can miss the characterization of Jesus in the gospels as fearless and courageous. He charges his followers to speak boldly without fear of reprisal (Mark 13:11). His enemies, though trying to lull him into a false sense of security, admit that he is a straight-shooter and does not court the favor of his hearers (Mark 12:14): "Teacher, we know that you are true, and care for no man; for you do not regard the position of men, but truly teach the way of God."

This brief survey is enough to sketch out the noble, sterling, and compassionate character of the Christian Savior as depicted in the gospels. No one will claim to find fault with such virtue. Even atheists and adherents of rival faiths will have to make only minor adjustments to take this character ideal for their own.

But now we will see that there is another aspect to the gospel portrait, one so anomalous that it is much easier simply to ignore it. We will not avert our eyes.

You have no doubt seen "red letter Bibles" that print the words of Jesus all in red. It seems plenty of people are reading Bibles with some of Jesus' words printed not in red, but in invisible ink! But we will venture to make them visible, so that it will no longer be possible to ignore them.

And in so doing, we must remember that Jesus presents himself as the spokesman for the divine Father. He permits no distance, no disagreement, between them. With this in mind, we turn next to a survey of the Father's character and deeds.

Notes

1. Chögyam Trungpa, *Cutting Through Spiritual Materialism* (Boston: Shambhala, 1987).

III

The Not-so-good Book

> Men occasionally stumble over the truth, but most of them pick
> themselves up and hurry off as if nothing ever happened.
>
> —Winston Churchill

Infallible Scripture, Fallible God?

No matter how many years you have attended church and heard weekly sermons, I dare say you will never have heard one on any of the Holy Bible's passages we will survey in this chapter. They all show God, Jehovah (not-quite-translated as "the Lord," or "the LORD" in most English Bibles) as being as brutal as any devil we can imagine.

But, despite the silence of sermons on them, few Bible-reading Christians remain unaware of these terrible texts. That would be pretty much impossible. Rather, pious readers encounter these verses with a resounding *thump*, scratch their heads in puzzlement, then turn the page to find a more amenable passage on which to meditate.

How to square these dismaying scripture passages with one's cherished picture of an adoring heavenly Father? They say, "Who knows? Chalk it up as one more problem God will elucidate one day when the roll is called up yonder."

You know, like predestination versus free will. Like how the heavenly Voice at Jesus' baptism could have said both "*You are* my beloved Son" (Mark 1:11) and "*This is* my beloved Son" (Matt. 3:17) at the same time. To this one adds—apparently without much disturbance to the placid surface of one's devotional adoration—God's merciless commands to Israelite soldiers to butcher Canaanite infants. Is *that* just some theological hiccup?

This oblivious callousness on the part of devout Christians is a prime case of trying to reduce *cognitive dissonance*. Once an esoteric term, this bit of jargon has become much more common in general discussion. That is because, once it is explained, it so well describes experiences everyone has had.

We experience cognitive dissonance when two of our beliefs clash, and we cannot manage to hold them both. A simple case would be "buyer's remorse." You buy a car, and soon it becomes evident it is a lemon. But you really hate to admit that. If you did, you'd have to face the fact that you're stuck with it and wasted your money. You hate the prospect of feeling like a fool.

So what do you do? You might tell yourself that the car's not really *that* bad, no matter how many parts of it fall off and bounce on the street. "Sure, there may be a few bugs here and there, but I'll work them out." Deep down, you know better, but you calculate you'd be better off repressing the truth. Suppose you discovered you had made a mistake when you married your spouse. Hoo boy! "Aw, she's not that bad, I guess. The guy she's having the affair with agrees!"

And what do you do if the book you have been taught and believe is the infallible Word of God tells you that God commanded genocide? Believers try to bracket the offensive verses and concentrate on the rest. They never notice what an unsound and unstable position they're putting themselves in.

What, you're going to believe and obey the verses that agree with your moral code and just disregard the ones that don't? Who's the "authority" here, the Bible or *you*? I'd say you don't even *need* the Bible. I'd say you don't have much of an advantage over the rest of us mere mortals who have to call 'em as we see 'em, with no pretense of infallibility. The Bible, then, after all, is no more infallible than your interpretation of it.

But there is a much more severe problem, one that accounts for the urgency of believers' efforts at reducing cognitive dissonance. A straightforward reading of the *whole Bible*–not just the parts they print on Bible bookmarks and in church bulletins–reveals God as totally incompatible with the Christian ethic on display in, e.g., the

Sermon on the Mount.

God is totally opposite to Jesus in the gospels, which we explored in the previous chapter. This is a God who is as offensive to our own moral conscience as the Trinity of Hitler-Stalin-Mao: a mad divinity! Something is awfully wrong! Indeed, we are seeing the clumsy hand of man here because God cannot be opposites: hate versus love. The First Epistle of John (4:8) assures us that "God is love." Meanwhile, the Old Testament pretty much says "God is hate." But he can't be both.

Jehovah's Jihad

As I write, Americans (to say nothing of those closer to the events) are much concerned, much alarmed, at an advancing tide of savagery and barbarism perpetrated in the name of Islam. The Caliphate, or Islamic State, helmed by one Abu-bakr al-Baghdadi, considers it their religious duty to conquer the world in the name of Islamic jihadism. All must live under the strictures of Shariah law. For them, all's fair in faith and war; thus, they commit mass crucifixions, beheadings, rapes, child murders, and sex-slave trading.

Yet the Christian holy scripture, the Bible, explicitly ascribes *the very same moral crimes* to God. Islamic Caliphate killers don't even need the Koran. There are hundreds of passages in the Holy Bible which would be more than enough to inspire their horrors. These are strong words, I know. I hate to have to write them. I hope you will have the courage to read them. It comes down to a question of your own integrity. I hope you will see that.

The butchers of the Caliphate consider it open season not only on non-Muslims, but also on Muslims who will not join them in their mayhem. But sometimes they allow Christians, Jews, Yezidis, and other "infidels" a choice: They can either (pretend to) convert to Islam or agree to live obediently under Shariah Law and pay a tax as second-class citizens.

In many places, however, God is by no means so lenient. The

Bible tells of the people of Israel, freed from Egyptian oppression, advancing on the numerous Canaanite tribes and petty kingdoms under orders from God to eradicate every single Canaanite. No treaties, no co-existence, no nothing. And let's be clear: it was purely and simply a matter of religion. The Canaanites had to be exterminated because they worshiped other deities.

Here are God's orders, as Samuel conveyed them to King Saul:

> Thus says the LORD of hosts, "I will punish what Amalek did to Israel in opposing them on the way, when they came up out of Egypt. Now go and smite Amalek, and utterly destroy all that they have; do not spare them, but kill both man and woman, infant and suckling, ox and sheep, camel and ass." (1 Sam. 15:2-3)

This passage presents an unequivocal command from God to Samuel and King Saul to wipe out 100% of an old pagan enemy. Okay, the time comes when a nation has to face down its enemies. But do you have to kill all the noncombatants? Talk about "collateral damage"!

In this policy of absolute annihilation, prefiguring the Nazi "Final Solution" of "the Jewish Problem," Saul and his patron Samuel were only following the custom established by Moses, who is depicted as fondly strolling down Memory Lane, reflecting on the blitzkriegs inflicted by his troops, at God's command, upon various heathen countries. "And we captured all his cities at that time and utterly destroyed every city, men, women, and children; we left none remaining." [Deut. 2:34]

King Og of Bashan received the same savage treatment: "And we utterly destroyed them, as we did to Sihon the king of Heshbon, destroying every city, men, women, and children. But all the cattle and the spoil of the cities we took as our booty" (Deut. 3:6-7). "So the LORD our God gave into our hand Og also, the king of Bashan, and all his people; and we smote him until no survivor was left to him" (Deut. 3:3).

Moses makes sure that his successors, who will press on into Canaan's Promised Land after he is no longer there to lead them, will pursue the same grisly tactics. "And when the LORD your God gives them over to you, and you defeat them; then you must utterly destroy them; you shall make no covenant with them, and show no mercy to them." (Deut. 7:2). And if it were not enough to put the pagan babies to the sword, let's not leave out those "unbelieving" pets and livestock!

> But in the cities of these peoples that the LORD your God gives you for an inheritance, you shall save alive nothing that breathes, but you shall utterly destroy them, the Hittites and the Amorites, the Canaanites and the Perizzites, the Hivites and the Jebusites, as the LORD your God has commanded. (Deut. 20:16-17)

Whatever other commandments the Israelites may have broken, they carried this one out to the letter. "Then they utterly destroyed all in the city, both men and women, young and old, oxen, sheep, and asses, with the edge of the sword" (Josh. 6:21). "For Joshua did not draw back his hand, with which he stretched out the javelin, until he had utterly destroyed all the inhabitants of Ai" (Josh. 8:26).

Joshua 10:28-40 recounts more of the same. It will not do to summarize it if we want to get the full effect.

> And Joshua took Makkedah on that day, and smote it and its king with the edge of the sword; he utterly destroyed every person in it, he left none remaining; and he did to the king of Makke'dah as he had done to the king of Jericho.
>
> Then Joshua passed on from Makkedah, and all Israel with him, to Libnah, and fought against Libnah; and the LORD gave it also and its king into the hand of Israel; and he smote it with the edge of the sword, and every person in it; he left none remaining in it; and he did to its king as he had done to the king of Jericho.

And Joshua passed on from Libnah, and all Israel with him, to Lachish, and laid siege to it, and assaulted it: and the Lord gave Lachish into the hand of Israel, and he took it on the second day, and smote it with the edge of the sword, and every person in it, as he had done to Libnah.

Then Horam king of Gezer came up to help Lachish; and Joshua smote him and his people, until he left none remaining.

And Joshua passed on with all Israel from Lachish to Eglon; and they laid siege to it, and assaulted it; and they took it on that day, and smote it with the edge of the sword; and every person in it he utterly destroyed that day, as he had done to Lachish.

Then Joshua went up with all Israel from Eglon to Hebron; and they assaulted it, and took it, and smote it with the edge of the sword, and its king and its towns, and every person in it; he left none remaining, as he had done to Eglon, and utterly destroyed it with every person in it.

Then Joshua, with all Israel, turned back to Debir and assaulted it, and he took it with its king and all its towns; and they smote them with the edge of the sword, and utterly destroyed every person in it; he left none remaining; as he had done to Hebron and to Libnah and its king, so he did to Debir and to its king.

So Joshua defeated the whole land, the hill country and the Negeb and the lowland and the slopes, and all their kings; he left none remaining, but utterly destroyed all that breathed, as the Lord God of Israel commanded.

If possible, it gets even worse in Numbers 31:17-18, where we read of God's rules of engagement: "Now therefore, kill every male among the little ones, and kill every woman who has known man by lying with him. But all the young girls who have not known man by lying with him, keep alive for yourselves."

Since we are used to reading with the prior assumption that Jehovah is the *real* God, *our* God, we tend to see little amiss here. But think about it: Why isn't it religious persecution pure and simple, no matter what god's name authorizes it? Why is it not like the mullahs of Iran killing off Baha'is? Why is it not like the Islamic State fanatics wiping out Shi'ites in Iraq?

What makes the Christian God any better than the God of Islam? Just the fact that one is in the Bible and the other isn't? If there's poison in the bottle, a different label doesn't make it any better.

Heresy and Apostasy

God didn't just order Israel to annihilate members of other religions outside of Israel. He had as little patience with any member of the Chosen People who converted to the worship of other deities or who still worshiped him but added other gods to the pantheon.

The visionary seer Ezekiel, writing during the Babylonian Exile, shares a revelation in which preparations are made for angels to slaughter all the inhabitants of Jerusalem who worship idols and gods such as the Sun, Ishtar, and Tammuz alongside Jehovah who is a jealous god unwilling to share his glory with another. The chief angel commands his six subordinates, "Pass through the city . . . , and smite; your eye shall not spare, and you shall show no pity; slay old men outright, young men and maidens, little children and women, but touch no one upon whom is the mark" that denotes God's faithful (Ezek. 9:5-6).

This is genocide, simply for having the wrong religion.

We hear of people condemned to execution in Pakistan or Saudi Arabia for the terrible crime of converting from Islam to Christianity or to secularism. Is it any different in Deuteronomy 13:5-9 (see just below)? Because we are rooting for the Bible's religion? As if passages like these might not be enough to make us question whether we ought to anymore?

But that prophet or that dreamer of dreams shall be put to death, because he has taught rebellion against the LORD your God, who brought you out of the land of Egypt and redeemed you out of the house of bondage, to make you leave the way in which the LORD your God commanded you to walk. So you shall purge the evil from the midst of you.

If your brother, the son of your mother, or your son, or your daughter, or the wife of your bosom, or your friend who is as your own soul, entices you secretly, saying, "Let us go and serve other gods," which neither you nor your fathers have known, some of the gods of the peoples that are round about you, whether near you or far off from you, from the one end of the earth to the other, you shall not yield to him or listen to him, nor shall your eye pity him, nor shall you spare him, nor shall you conceal him; but you shall kill him; your hand shall be first against him to put him to death, and afterwards the hand of all the people. (Deut. 13:5-9)

Not all the atrocities of the Bible are wrought by human agents acting on God's commands. Sometimes he reaches down directly into the mortal world, as in the Exodus narrative.

It is common to draw a parallel between Matthew's episode of King Herod's Slaughter of the Innocents in Bethlehem and Pharaoh's attempt to eliminate the Hebrew nation by ordering the midwives to kill all male Hebrew babies. It is a true parallel, but another parallel is always ignored. Pharaoh's scheme fails, and years later, when Moses demands that he release Israel, who is God's own son, Pharaoh refuses. God then announces that he will retaliate in kind: If Pharaoh will not allow God's firstborn son to leave in peace, then God will deprive all Egypt of their firstborn, human and animal.

At midnight the LORD smote all the first-born in the land of Egypt, from the first-born of Pharaoh who sat on his throne to the first-born of the captive who was in the dungeon, and all the first-born of the cattle. And Pharaoh rose up in the night, he, and all his servants, and all the Egyptians; and there was a great cry in Egypt, for there was not a house where one was not dead. (Exod. 12:29-30)

I should say that this part of the story is an even better parallel between Exodus and Matthew, only it is God himself who is the Old Testament counterpart to the evil King Herod. He wants to get back at one man, Pharaoh, so he slaughters great numbers of innocent Egyptians, just as Herod wants to eliminate one particular Jewish baby and kills all the babies of Bethlehem to do it. Stalin famously quipped, "You can't make an omelet without breaking eggs." Well, that's one hell of an omelet!

Weaseling Out of It

Now, most Bible readers are at least vaguely aware of these pogroms against pagans and polytheists, and some find it something of a problem. But the real problem for them is the public relations disaster these texts present for their belief in the infallibility of scripture. Why do they not recognize the true moral horror on display in the Conquest narratives?

I think it is because they subconsciously still regard the stories as they did when they first heard them in Sunday school. They do not think of the Canaanites as people, human beings whose chief crime was belonging to non-Jehovah religions. Instead, they view them as story-book villains like Sauron's army of Orcs in *The Lord of the Rings*. Of course! *Every one* of them was a devil! It was good that Moses and Joshua killed all of them, like Professor Van Helsing (in Bram Stoker's *Dracula*) staking every single vampire he finds.

Christian readers of the Bible (at least some of them) do seem to ponder why God would allow, much less command, such horrors. But that is not good enough. If you are asking yourself, "How could my God, the true God, do such things?" you are stopping short of the real question. It is this: "Why should I believe that a God who issues such orders is more than a tribal totem embodying and justifying the bloodlust and hatreds of an ancient people? How can

I, with any shred of conscience, profess allegiance to such a figure?"

"But biblical morality and biblical God-concepts grew more sophisticated as time went on," it is all too tempting to say in reply. "Israel gradually came to a clearer picture of the Deity." That is no doubt correct. But don't you see what that means? It means that what we are seeing in the Bible is the evolution of a man-made religion. There remains no more reason to consider the Bible a revelation from a God who knows better than poor, primitive mortals.

You can readily acknowledge that the *post*-biblical development of Christian belief and practice (from Tertullian to Augustine to Anselm to Aquinas to Luther and Calvin, etc.) was a ricocheting echo chamber of human opinions and ideas. But there you can *afford* to, because no one is asking you to believe that the opinions of all these theologians came straight from the all-knowing Creator of the Universe.

What if you are willing to discount those passages in which God commands genocide and infanticide as merely the biases of primitive worshipers of a God whose loving nature is clearer to us moderns? Then plainly you must realize that, even if scripture explicitly says, "God commanded so-and-so," that doesn't mean he did. Don't you realize you're admitting the Bible was mistaken? And then, how do you know when it's *not* mistaken? I come back to my point: Your judgment is your authority, not the Bible, which many seem to "believe" only when they agree with it.

And that's nothing to be ashamed of! The only thing to be ashamed of is hiding behind the supposed authority of the Bible to buttress your own opinions. If you have the courage of your convictions, surely you should be able to present to another person the solid reasons that led you to think as you do. Assuming there *were* any real reasons.

If you were raised believing in the murderous faith of the Islamic Caliphate, you might have qualms about some of the things your leaders said Allah had commanded, but you'd be looking at things from the inside, and you'd chalk it up to "one of those divine mysteries." But you are, thankfully, viewing their atrocities from outside, so you have no difficulty recognizing the horrors of a death cult for what they are.

The presence of these awful verses in the Old Testament does not make Christianity a death cult. That's not my point. But this is: If the Old Testament Jehovah is portrayed as the blood-spattered totem of a slaughter cult, it is high time you stepped out of the Bible bubble for an objective look at it. It is time you decided if you really belong there.

A Good God?

At this point, God's defenders often resort to *equivocation*. They like to point out that God is so astronomically far above us that it's futile for us to imagine "good" meaning the same thing for him as it does for us. We say "Good dog!" when Fido refrains from wetting the living room carpet. That has little in common with what we mean when we say "Dr. King was a good man."

But isn't there actually a degree of continuity between them? Our pet's "goodness" is just on a much lower level, we might venture to say. So why should we find it difficult to learn Job's lesson, that God cannot be held to *our* standards, *our* Fido-like definitions of good and evil?

It's a nice try, but I'm afraid it doesn't work. True, the idea of "good" must have a much wider scope and more dimensions for Almighty God than it does for us, but if we want to extend God's "goodness" so far that it winds up looking just like our "evil," then words have become completely meaningless.

Say that a deity who commands genocide, religious persecution, and the abduction of virgins is nonetheless "good" if you want to. But then you will just be spewing pious gibberish. God's ostensible goodness is no longer any guide to what we may expect from him. Oh yes, he's "good," thank goodness, but that doesn't mean he won't victimize or exterminate the innocent. *Whatever* he did, the pious apologist has ready excuses for his God. "He's all-righteous, so he must have *some* good reason for it!" If you woke up in hell one fine morning, despite your Christian faith and God's promise that it would save you, I guess you'd have to conclude he must know what he's doing.

Ours is not to reason why; ours is but to boil and fry. Maybe so, but why empty the word "good" of what we all mean and understand by it by applying it to such a being?

Sin Versus Spin

Again, most Christians find themselves baffled, even embarrassed, by the divine atrocities of the Old Testament. Very few, I feel sure, actually embrace Jehovah's ruthlessness and intolerance ("I, Jehovah, am a jealous God"). Those who do, like the Medieval Crusaders, the witch-burners, the anti-Semites, and the Westboro Baptists, are being, dare I say it, *consistent*. These, like Muslim Jihadists, have had the guts to recognize the barbarism of their scripture's deity and to build it into their ethics.

If we are to take our god as our moral paragon, without cutting him down to our own size, without redrawing him in our own morally superior (or squeamish) image, we must dare to emulate him. Otherwise, what's the point? This is why a concept of God that contains the elements of mercilessness and cruelty is positively dangerous. We must not be surprised if the worshipers of an intolerant God behave with intolerance themselves.

But even if we silently weed out the primitive and the reprehensible, there remains a quite different moral danger. Here I am thinking of a provocative scene in Dostoyevsky's great novel *The Brothers Karamazov*. Two brothers meet to talk. One, Alyosha, is a pious churchman. The other, Ivan, has not darkened the door of a church for years. Alyosha makes a last-ditch effort to reclaim his brother's soul. Won't he come back into the welcoming arms of Mother Church? Ivan refuses and explains. He cannot bring himself to endorse a God who would stand by and do nothing to stop the suffering of innocent children.

Now, suppose Ivan were to swallow his objections, telling himself, "Well, God must have some good reason for not helping them." Then he would be saying God's impassive indifference is just fine with him. God would be no less guilty, but now Ivan would have become an accomplice after the fact. Is a ticket to heaven worth the price of one's own integrity?

Ivan was unwilling to save his soul by losing it. Are you?

Good Cop, Bad Cop?

What, you may be asking, is the connection between this chapter and the previous one where we praised a merciful Jesus? There we reviewed the features of Jesus' character that make him so attractive. Here, we have put on display the repellent and immoral features of Jehovah in the Old Testament.

I believe that many Christians, conservative as well as liberal, think (albeit vaguely) that the New Testament either exonerates the God of the Old or just plain renders him irrelevant. This is very strange if you profess to believe that both Testaments are the inspired Word of God.

My considered guess is that they are thinking of the Pauline notion that Christ and his gospel have superseded the Torah, the Old Testament Law. But that is quite a different matter. Paul says that the *ceremonial* provisions of Judaism (circumcision, kosher laws, holy days, etc.) are no longer binding since their proper purpose has been fulfilled as of the coming of Christ (Col. 2:16-17; Gal. 2:15-21; Rom. 10:4). But that has nothing to do with *genocide*, as if something so morally repugnant could be proper in the Old Testament dispensation but not in the New.

But, hey, who wants to look too closely? If you're looking for an excuse to sweep Old Testament atrocities under the rug, any old broom will do.

The contrast between the Old Testament God and his New

Testament Son is no new discovery. Christians have pondered it, on and off, for many centuries. Some ancient Christians, stigmatized as "heretics" by the Church authorities, took a pretty direct approach.

The second-century Marcionites held that Jesus was not the Son of the Old Testament God, a deity of rough justice and little mercy. Rather, Jesus had been sent into the world by *a different God altogether*, a loving and forgiving Father who judges no one. They just couldn't figure any way to reconcile the Testaments and their respective deities.

Is this the answer? I'd say that it's pretty radical surgery, and virtually no Christians today are willing to pay those medical bills! Dare one split asunder the divine Trinity? If not, what is left to us?

If we cherish the Trinity, we might as well get used to the fact that *Jesus bears the blame for Jehovah's crimes*–because Jesus *is* Jehovah and the Father and the Lord. But you needn't go so far as to say that Jesus is the Father (even though, as we have seen, some gospel passages imply it). The Father by himself is not Jehovah; the *Trinity* is Jehovah. And this means that *Jesus is Jehovah.* Our picture of Jesus looks quite different once we factor in the Trinity.

In the next chapter we will take another look at the Jesus of the gospels. We will see that perhaps the contrast between gentle Jesus and genocidal Jehovah is not so stark after all.

IV

Lord of Damnation

> In the old testament, when God got a man dead, He let him alone. When He saw him quietly in his grave He was satisfied. The muscles relaxed, and a smile broke over the Divine face. But in the new testament the trouble commences just at death. In the new testament God is to wreak His revenge forever and ever. It was reserved for one who said, "Love your enemies," to tear asunder the veil between time and eternity and fix the horrified gaze of men upon the gulfs of eternal fire. The new testament is just as much worse than the old, as hell is worse than sleep; just as much worse as infinite cruelty is worse than annihilation; and yet, the new testament is pointed to as a gospel of love and peace.
>
> —Robert G. Ingersoll, *Lecture on Orthodoxy*

It comes as quite a shock to discover that, according to Christian theology, the sweet Savior Jesus Christ–embodiment of mercy and compassion, friend of the lowly and the oppressed–was the incarnation of the very God who, in the Old Testament, ordered genocide, religious persecution, and enslavement, and who received human sacrifices. How could it be? Had the old deity mellowed, even repented, in the meantime? That cannot be if "there is no variation or shadow due to change" in him (James 1:17), if he "is the same yesterday and today and forever" (Heb. 13:8). Does the Son of God, the Second Person of the Trinity, come as a false prophet, bringing false tidings of "'Peace!' 'Peace!' when there is no peace" (Jer. 6:14; 8:11)? There appears at first to be a yawning chasm between Jehovah in the Old Testament and Jesus in the New.

But perhaps not.

There is certainly a gross inconsistency, a fatal and fundamental contradiction, before us. What if it is an unstable fault line running through the gospel portrait of Jesus Christ himself? He teaches a message of love, mercy, and forgiveness, yet he's also found to be teaching the very opposite.

As we have seen, Jesus depicts God as a loving Father who may be relied upon to be at least as generous and attentive as any earthly father:

> What man of you, if his son asks him for a loaf, will give him a stone? Or if he asks for a fish will give him a serpent? If you then, who are evil, know how to give gifts to your children, how much more will your Father who is in heaven give good things to those who ask him? (Matt. 7:9-11)

But he also assures us that God is planning to treat not just some but most of his children (Luke 13:23-27) in a truly dreadful manner. So horribly, in fact, that it is impossible to imagine any mortal father treating his children that way—unless, perhaps, he were an insane sadist.

In some sayings, much in the vein of the Book of Proverbs, Jesus warns his hearers to take stock of themselves and their habits lest they find their lives ruined. "Enter by the narrow gate; for the gate is wide and the way is easy that leads to destruction, and those who enter by it are many. For the gate is narrow and the way is hard, that leads to life, and those who find it are few" (Matt. 7:13-14).

There is no threat here, not a hint of some punishment imposed by God. No, the point is that certain actions must inevitably lead to destructive consequences. Alcoholism, smoking, and drug addiction would be prime examples. It is not as if God just doesn't happen to like these things, so he sets a high price tag on them. God doesn't punish you for smoking by giving you cancer; no, smoking is wrong (at least ill-advised) because it will in and of itself give you cancer.

But I am not talking about such prudential warnings from a wise man. Rather, I refer to Jesus' threats of hellfire, conscious suffering in an afterlife of endless torture, imposed by God.

We read nothing about hell in the Old Testament. There is barely an intimation of *any* afterlife in the Old Testament. Robert Green Ingersoll saw this: "Now, in the Old Testament there is not, in my judgment, a single reference to another life." [1] We do read of a vague and shadowy half-existence in "Sheol" ("the Pit"), but there is nothing said about either suffering or punishment.

The wicked and the righteous alike wind up in Sheol. In fact, Sheol often seems like a mere metaphor for being dead, period, and some Old Testament texts speak only of "returning to the dust" or "to the ground" (Gen. 3:19; Eccl. 3:18-20). Eventually we read in Isaiah 26:19 and Daniel 12:2 of martyrs for their faith being rewarded one day by a resurrection of the dead. But there is no roast for the wicked.

It is *Jesus* who introduces hell into the Bible. He does not announce it as some new revelation. Sometime between the Old and the New Testament the belief had become widespread. Ingersoll was correct as to its origin: "Do you know nobody would have had an idea of hell in this world if it hadn't been for volcanoes? They were looked upon as the chimneys of hell. The idea of eternal fire never would have polluted the imagination of man but for them." [2]

Specifically, it appears that we owe the doctrine of a fiery, subterranean hell to ancient Pythagorean missionaries fanning out across the Mediterranean world from Sicily, where the magma pits, volcanoes, hot springs, and fumaroles had seared themselves into the religious imagination. All these things they viewed as "hell mouths" on earth. [7]

Pretty Damned Important
Late Warnings about Eternity

What difference does any of this make? There are two very important points. First, if hell was always real, and a real destination for the damned, why are we so late in hearing anything about it? If the stakes are that high, don't you think it would have been sporting of God to let everyone know of the danger they faced? Yet he was utterly silent on the topic until Jesus came along.

In Old Testament Israel, about the worst a sinner had to fear was leaving a bad reputation behind. And if you really wanted to do some mischief, well, that might not be much of a deterrent! Sure, let 'em badmouth you—who cares? You wouldn't be there to hear it!

But if you knew you faced the prospect of never-ending torment, well, you might think twice! After all, that's the way it's been preached for at least a couple of thousand years now.

Second, if Jesus did not *reveal* the existence of hell, but merely bought into the popular religious beliefs of his day about it, we have to wonder if the whole notion of hell was like the belief that the sun orbited the earth. And if Jesus shared such assumptions, what kind of revealer, what sort of divine authority, was he?

The more problems we uncover with Jesus' teachings on hell, the more sense it makes to write it off as a mere human invention. Remember "man-made" looks very much like "madman" shuffled around a bit. And you don't need to live your life in fear of the delusions of a madman.

Bearer of Bad Tidings

John's gospel depicts Jesus as saying, "For God sent his Son into the world, not to condemn the world, but that the world might be saved through him" (John 3:17). Is that so? We might get a different impression when we consider some more of Jesus' sayings from the gospels.

Mark 9:43-48 has Jesus warn his hearers to cut their losses: Repentance may require radical surgery, but it's a whole lot better than flailing around in hell!

> And if your hand causes you to sin, cut it off; it is better for you to enter life maimed than with two hands to go to hell, to the unquenchable fire. And if your foot causes you to sin, cut it off; it is better for you to enter life lame than with two feet to be thrown into hell. And if your eye causes you to sin, pluck it out; it is better for you to enter the kingdom of God with one eye than with two eyes to be thrown into hell, where their worm does not die and the fire is not quenched.

Is Jesus suggesting literal self-mutilation? Given ancient (and even modern!) Middle Eastern culture, that's not out of the question. Convicted thieves in Saudi Arabia have their hands amputated, the punishment thus fitting the crime. But we don't have to read it that way.

Even in modern Aramaic (a version of the language spoken by Jesus),[8] we find the idiom of "cutting off the offending hand." Catching your neighbor about to steal your lawnmower, you might say, "Hey! Cut off your hand from my mower!" It's the same as when we say, "Hands off my mower!" The same applies to "cutting off the offending foot," only this implies trespassing, going where you have no business. "Plucking out the eye" obviously refers to averting the lustful gaze.

In any case, it might be quite difficult to break bad habits, but if you don't, there will be hell to pay. But how *literal* a hell? Even if do-it-yourself amputation is not the point, the hell business is still wildly extreme. Recognizing metaphors for changing your evil ways isn't going to take the sting out of hell.

Some contend that Jesus is not talking about conscious postmortem punishment at all. The word translated "hell" is actually a place name, *Gehenna*, or "the Valley of the Sons of Hinnom," also known as *Tophet* (Jer. 7:31-32; 2 Kings 23:10). The theory says that this was the site of a rubbish dump at the foot of Mount Zion, the Temple Mount. Into it would have been tossed the carcasses of ritually unclean animals (pigs, etc.) and corpses of notorious sinners whose infamy made it impossible for them to receive a decent burial. In this case, we are told, Jesus' warning would amount to "Clean up your act, or you may be found unworthy of burial in sacred ground!"

This understanding of the passage would sound quite reasonable, except that, as far as we know, the interpretation goes back no further than commentator Rabbi David Kimchi (1160–1235).[9] Though attested so late, it still might be true except for the fact that archaeology shows no evidence of garbage ever being burned at the site.

At any rate, by New Testament times "Gehenna" did denote a postmortem place of torment. I'd say this reading is clinched by the repeated reference to the undying maggots and the never-failing fire. What's the point of highlighting the duration of these if not to denote the unending experience of these awful things?

I have heard effective sermons on this passage by more liberally inclined clergymen, pointing out that we make our own "living hells" by indulging our self-destructive habits. That is a profound application of the text. But I think that is what it is: an *application*, a transposition of the verses into another key: that of psychology rather than theology. So you can see the "garbage dump" idea of hell is just a futile attempt to get Jesus off the hook. We hate to think of him teaching hell-fire torment, so we look for a less sadistic alternative. "Yeah, *that's* the ticket!"

Sorry, but it is hard to evade the truth that Jesus is shown here predicting hellfire for those who do not repent while there's still time. You might call it killing a mouse with an elephant gun; the behaviors he lists (stealing, trespassing, ogling) would seem to carry their own "punishments" by their intrinsic nature and their likely social repercussions, like the fate of an adulterer caught in the act by his lover's husband (Prov. 6:23-29, 32-35; 7:6-27).

Do you really need additional threats of never-ending torment amid flames and devouring worms on top of real-world blow-back? If you think you do, if you think it is best to frighten people out of negative behavior, you are short-circuiting the growth of moral sensitivity and mature conscience.

And a Jesus who tried to scare the hell out of people (or to scare them out of hell!) wouldn't be much of a moral teacher, despite his reputation. He would be holding you back in the most infantile stage of morality: keeping your hand out of the cookie jar for fear of a whipping.

But that's what he does. In Matthew 18:23-35, for example, he offers a parable on forgiveness that carries a surprising sting in its tail:

Therefore the kingdom of heaven may be compared to a king who wished to settle accounts with his servants. When he began the reckoning, one was brought to him who owed him ten thousand talents; and as he could not pay, his lord ordered him to be sold, with his wife and children and all that he had, and payment to be made. So the servant fell on his knees, imploring him, "Lord, have patience with me, and I will pay you everything." And out of pity for him the lord of that servant released him and forgave him the debt.

But that same servant, as he went out, came upon one of his fellow servants who owed him a hundred denarii; and seizing him by the throat he said, "Pay what you owe." So his fellow servant fell down and besought him, "Have patience with me, and I will pay you." He refused and went and put him in prison till he should pay the debt. When his fellow servants saw what had taken place, they were greatly distressed, and they went and reported to their lord all that had taken place.

Then his lord summoned him and said to him, "You wicked servant! I forgave you all that debt because you besought me; and should not you have had mercy on your fellow servant, as I had mercy on you?" And in anger his lord delivered him to the jailers, till he should pay all his debt. So also my heavenly Father will do to every one of you, if you do not forgive your brother from your heart.

The threat here could not be more explicit—except for one thing, the matter of how Bible translators try to soften the blow. Did Jesus warn the unforgiving that they might end up in the custody of "the jailers"? No, the Greek word in the original text actually means "*torturers*." Yikes! The metaphor underlying the whole parable is that of being hauled off to debtor's prison.

As Oscar Madison put it in an episode of *The Odd Couple*, "It's *bail* before *jail* so you'd better not *fail!*" You couldn't pay your debts? All right. There are other ways to pay it. You would languish in prison (like poor John the Baptist in the dungeon of Herod Antipas) until your relatives, spurred by a new sense of urgency, begged, borrowed, or stole the money you owed. To redouble their zeal, the authorities might put you under torture, taking it out of your hide.

And this, Jesus says, is what God will do to . . . child molesters? Rapists? Mass murderers? No, he's talking about *real* felons: those too stubborn to forgive. Nowadays we point out to such people that they need to forgive for their own sakes; otherwise it will warp and twist them, eat them up inside. But Jesus bypasses all that touchy-feely stuff. He goes right for the jugular, threatening you with torture in hell. Nice.

And who exactly might these torturers *be*? In the Bible we never quite get to the medieval notion of red, horned demons twisting hot pokers in the innards of those sentenced to hell. But, come to think of it, are we so very far from that?

Matthew 13:41-42 suggests that it is angels who will be assigned to the task. "The Son of man will send his angels, and they will gather out of his kingdom all causes of sin and all evildoers, and throw them into the furnace of fire; there men will weep and gnash their teeth." Ditto Matthew 13:49-50: "So it will be at the close of the age. The angels will come out and separate the evil from the righteous, and throw them into the furnace of fire; there men will weep and gnash their teeth."

A touch of local color is added to hell, Gehenna, which is here described as "the furnace of fire." Does that phrase remind you of anything? Like maybe the ovens in which Hitler incinerated his Jewish captives?

Hellocaust

I remember many years ago when my young daughter and I were watching a TV show about World War Two. Some Hitler footage came on the screen, and I pointed to him and said to little Victoria, "See that man? That's the most evil man who ever lived." If there is anyone you even might think belongs in a hell of eternal torture, it would be *der Führer*, right?

And yet the Bible tells us (and Jesus tells us), so to speak, that someone worse than Adolf *runs* the place! *Jawohl*, God routinely does something the fiendish Hitler could only have dreamed of doing: consigning untold billions of victims to an *eternity* of tongue-gnawing agony in his furnace where the fire is never quenched. And for what crime? Same one: being Jews–or anything other than Christian believers.

Look carefully at Matthew 25:41-46, a very famous passage always quoted in the service of the Social Gospel:

> When the Son of man comes in his glory, and all the angels with him, then he will sit on his glorious throne. Before him will be gathered all the nations, and he will separate them one from another as a shepherd separates the sheep from the goats, and he will place the sheep at his right hand, but the goats at the left.

> Then the King will say to those at his right hand, "Come, O blessed of my Father, inherit the kingdom prepared for you from the foundation of the world; for I was hungry and you gave me food, I was thirsty and you gave me drink, I was a stranger and you welcomed me, I was naked and you clothed me, I was sick and you visited me, I was in prison and you came to me."

> Then the righteous will answer him, "Lord, when did we see thee hungry and feed thee, or thirsty and give thee drink? And when did we see thee a stranger and welcome thee, or naked and clothe thee? And when did we see thee sick or in prison and visit thee?" And the King will answer them, "Truly, I say to you, as you did it to one of the least of these my brethren, you did it to me."

> Then he will say to those at his left hand, "Depart from me, you cursed, into the eternal fire prepared for the devil and

> his angels; for I was hungry and you gave me no food, I was thirsty and you gave me no drink, I was a stranger and you did not welcome me, naked and you did not clothe me, sick and in prison and you did not visit me."
>
> Then they also will answer, "Lord, when did we see thee hungry or thirsty or a stranger or naked or sick or in prison, and did not minister to thee?"
>
> Then he will answer them, "Truly, I say to you, as you did it not to one of the least of these, you did it not to me." And they will go away into eternal punishment, but the righteous into eternal life.

The destination of the "goats" is pretty clear: They are to share the fate of the devil and his fallen angels. But what was their damning offense? Perhaps not what you think! We are used to hearing that the "goats" were callous toward the plight of society's downtrodden, whom they could have helped but did not (a theme we *will* see in the story of the Rich Man and Lazarus, just below). Such cold indifference is indeed a serious offense, though we still might wonder if it deserves eternal torment.

But I don't think that is quite what is going on in the parable. In the context of Matthew's gospel as a whole, it seems more likely that the damned are those "nations" into whose midst Jesus is shown sending his apostles to preach the gospel of the kingdom of God. They are to go out by faith, trusting in God to provide for their needs through the generosity of their hearers, exactly like the wandering Buddhist monks in Southeast Asia today. Pious laymen gain merit by giving food to the monks when they come knocking at the door. Kind of a religious Trick-or-Treat.

The plight described by the Son of Man is that of his wandering "brethren," the missionaries.[10] The goats' neglect of these missionaries' needs means they turned a deaf ear to their gospel preaching. Had they believed, they would have provided shelter and food, exactly as the Philippian convert Lydia does in Acts 16:14-15. This means that the "goats" are damned for slamming the door in the faces of Jesus' Witnesses. They have refused the Christian gospel, not merely failed to help the generic homeless. The "sheep," of course, are those nations who accepted the Christian faith.

Again, some try to get Jesus off the hook by suggesting that he may not be saying that the billygoats gruff will be tormented forever, but only that an eternally blazing fire will instantly reduce them to ashes (which does, I'll admit, sound more merciful than the alternative!). But this would make the description of the fire as "eternal" pointless. It pretty much has to refer to the endless duration of the torture. The damned will be weeping and gnashing their splintering teeth *forever* as the flames lick their asbestos hides. After all, it does say "eternal punishment."

Luke 16:19-26 gives us the parable of the Rich Man and Lazarus:

> There was a rich man, who was clothed in purple and fine linen and who feasted sumptuously every day. And at his gate lay a poor man named Lazarus, full of sores, who desired to be fed with what fell from the rich man's table; moreover the dogs came and licked his sores. The poor man died and was carried by the angels to Abraham's bosom.

> The rich man also died and was buried; and in Hades, being in torment, he lifted up his eyes, and saw Abraham far off and Lazarus in his bosom. And he called out, "Father Abraham, have mercy upon me, and send Lazarus to dip the end of his finger in water and cool my tongue; for I am in anguish in this flame."

> But Abraham said, "Son, remember that you in your lifetime received your good things, and Lazarus in like manner evil things; but now he is comforted here, and you are in anguish. And besides all this, between us and you a great chasm has been fixed, in order that those who would pass from here to you may not be able, and none may cross from there to us."

By now we are not surprised to read that the wicked Rich Man, who could so easily have helped the homeless beggar Lazarus, is suffering torment in a pit of supernatural flames, just as the gospel-rejecting nations are doomed to do in Matthew 25:41-46, just above. This man's sin *was* a "social" one, telling Lazarus, "Beat it, ya bum!"

But let's not miss the shocking hypocrisy of God–that's who Father Abraham stands for, of course. The Rich Man is roasting on Hades' spit and pleads for mercy, and not even for very *much* mercy. He's not asking for a day off once in a while, or for Cable TV in his cell.

All the Plutocrat in Pluto's realm is asking is that God might send Lazarus to visit him and drip a little water onto his crisping tongue! Nope, sorry, God says. Tough luck–you should have thought of that before, when you could have fed the starving Lazarus. And the parable is explicit that such refusal to succor the tormented of hell is *standard policy*! A policy of unforgiveness–the very trait for which people are damned in Matthew 18:23-35! Looks like two wrongs make a right!

Again, did not Ingersoll have a sharper insight than the theologians?

> We are taught to love our enemies, to pray for those that persecute us, to forgive. Should not the merciful God practice what he preaches? I say that reverently. Why should he say "Forgive your enemies" if he will not himself forgive? Why should he say "Pray for those that despise and persecute you, but if they refuse to believe my doctrine I will burn them forever?" I cannot believe it.[3]

And why *does* anyone believe it? Isn't it obvious? Christians have been cowed, bullied, terrorized into believing it lest they themselves go to hell for rejecting "biblical truth."

The Final Exam

There's an old joke where Junior spots his grandfather sitting on a park bench, Bible open on his lap and studying religious tracts. This seems uncharacteristic for the old man. So Junior goes home and asks Mommy what her dad's doing. Her answer: "Grampa's cramming for his finals!" Some of the best theology, I find, is in jokes. This one certainly hits the nail on the head.

Christian believers insist that salvation is based on "faith" in God, in Christ. But there is a fatal ambiguity in this tenet. They like to claim that, while Judaism, Hinduism and the rest are mere "religions," Christianity by contrast is "a relationship" with God and Christ. Some sort of personal encounter. But they say that this relationship presupposes several "facts" about God, e.g., that God is a Trinity of Father, Son, and Spirit, and that he has revealed himself, his will, and his promises of salvation in scripture. You see, he was kind enough to want to spare us a lot of fruitless guesswork.

Thus, barely hidden in the rhetoric of personal encounter with Christ, there is a pretty detailed set of theological beliefs required of anyone who would be saved. Suppose a new convert were to confide in his pastor that he had accepted Jesus Christ as his personal savior but just could not accept the doctrine of the Trinity or the inspiration of the Bible. He would at once be told this is impossible. To reject these pieces of theology is to reveal the counterfeit character of his "faith." All *real* Christians believe in the Trinity and the Bible. Thus, it's *not* just "faith alone" that saves, not by a long shot.

Granted, accepting these items on the theological checklist is not sufficient by itself for salvation (for "even the demons believe, and shudder"–James 2:19). You still have to enter into that "personal relationship with Christ," but accepting the tenets of the creed turns out to be a necessary prerequisite. It's the "fine print," you see. It's not just the devil that's in the details; God's there, too.

As Ingersoll said: "The fact is, that you have got not merely to believe the Bible, but you must also believe in a certain interpretation of it, and, mind you, you must also believe in the doctrine of the Trinity." [4] Thus "salvation by faith, not by works," turns out to be a sham. One is really trying to be saved by *cognitive works*,[11] believing in a whole party platform of doctrines, and that by sheer force of will.

Could this possibly be what the Savior, the one whose yoke was easy and his burden light, had in mind? You bet! Listen to his words. "You will die in your sins unless you believe that I am he" (John 8:24). "For God so loved the world that he gave his only Son, that whoever believes in him should not perish but have eternal life" (John 3:16). "He who believes and is baptized will be saved; he who does not believe will be condemned" (Mark 16:16).[12]

It is not that Jesus says that merely "signing on the dotted line" will convey salvation. He has plenty to say about the dangers of hypocrisy, the contradiction of professed beliefs by incongruous deeds. But good deeds mean nothing without the required creed. That is what it finally comes down to: By creed and deed art thou freed.

In the remote days of my youth, I once heard the famous campus evangelist Paul Little field a crucial question. A student asked him if he thought Mahatma Gandhi was saved and in heaven. Little's spin-doctor answer was, "Yes, provided he accepted Jesus Christ as his savior as he lay on his deathbed." And what, we might wonder, are the chances of *that*?

Of course Gandhi lived one of the most "Christlike" lives of any human being. He loved and lived the Sermon on the Mount. But he did not abandon his ancestral Hinduism, nor did he see any need to do so. But that meant nothing to this Christian apologist. It was fine with him to number Gandhi among the transgressors, to relegate him to the cosmic barbecue pit along with Ku Klux Klan members, profane wife-beaters, drug-pushers, Jihadist terrorists and Nazis– because (unlike many of them) he did not affirm the Christian creed.

Christians feel they have no other choice than to say this, as horrible as it sounds even to them, for if they allowed good works into the equation, they would be destroying the gospel of "faith alone." If we admit Gandhi must have been saved, aren't we saying

God judges by works rather than by (the correct) faith? But no one is saying that Gandhi was trying, in his costly advocacy of the Indian Untouchables, to win passage to heaven, like a kid trying to win a free vacation by selling magazine subscriptions. I daresay Gandhi had not a single thought for his own salvation; he was too busy helping others to have time for that.

The point is: Will God condemn the righteous simply because they do not belong to a particular religious club? Well, if he does, it becomes obvious that the criterion of salvation is getting an "A" on that final exam, after all. Christians themselves can smell something wrong there, and so in trying to explain what they "really" believe, they keep hopping from one foot ("It's all about faith in Jesus") to the other ("Works are necessary, too, but, er, only as outward signs of a genuine faith"), and back again.

Feudal and Futile

Anselm's attempt at explaining things

Why can't God simply forgive the sins of mankind, or of individuals within it? Some vital questions arise here. First, why would, how *could*, any act, major or minor, committed by a human being resonate so loudly that eternal torture could be considered a fit punishment?

The tenth-century theologian Anselm of Canterbury has the distinction of coming up with the only sensible explanation for this–and even *it* does not make any sense! He invoked the principles of then-current feudal justice whereby the same offense carried greater or lesser gravity depending on the greater or lesser degree of "honor" possessed by the one offended.

Imagine yourself a miserable peasant, a serf enjoying the protection of the Lord of the Manor in exchange for your service to him, including a share of your crops. Times are hard, and you steal a sheep from his already-scant flock. If you are found out, you have to reimburse him. Not that big a deal. But suppose that instead you snatch a sheep from the Lord of the Manor's large herd and are discovered. It could be capital punishment!

Why? Not because of any inherent severity of the crime. The Lord of the Manor isn't going to be particularly deprived by the loss of one lousy sheep. You need it far more than he does. The thing is, you have dared to commit an offense against a personage of far greater honor, and this increases the price of your transgression. Robbing some *schlumpf*? Bah, just a tempest in a teapot! But robbing the Lord of the Manor, the guy with the big castle and the nice clothes? Now *that* is the crime of the century.

So, the reasoning goes, if a feudal lord carries such gravity, imagine the severity of an offense against the Almighty Lord of the universe! *Any* offense against him has eternal repercussions, because you have wounded his infinite honor, his divine majesty! This is why any sin, no matter how humanly insignificant, is eternally significant in the cosmic scheme of things.

How does all this relate to the chief sin in Christian reckoning, namely rejecting belief in Christ and his plan of salvation? Imagine you, a peasant, receive an engraved invitation to join the king at his banqueting table, a scarcely imaginable daydream. But you get the invitation and you RSVP with this: "Thanks, Your Majesty, but I've got better things to do."

Watch it, buddy—you'd better not blow off the king like that! He can't let a slight like that pass without reprisals, or he's going to lose honor, lose face in the eyes of his subjects and his enemies. He must show he is not to be trifled with!

This is precisely why, in Jesus' parable of the Great Supper (Matt. 22:1-10), the king sends troops to destroy those who spurned his invitation to his son's wedding feast. Jesus' warning is directed to his hearers who are in danger of making the same mistake by declining his gospel invitation. To quote Paul, "God is not mocked!" (Gal. 6:7).

You see, the hell doctrine takes for granted feudal justice, with the disproportionate severity of the same offense against persons of greater and lesser honor. "We all agree that this is right and just, don't we? Then how can it be wrong to understand God acting the same way?"

It *is* wrong, because our idea of justice is very different–yes, far better–than what was practiced in the flickering light of the dark ages. Anselm's notion appears grotesque to us now, and rightly so. It's almost like saying, "If the commandant of Dachau is entitled to do so-and-so, then it must be all right for God to do it, too."

In addition, this "honor/shame" business [13] is grossly inappropriate when applied to God, and precisely *because* of the unimaginable superiority of his divine dignity. Can God be so petty? Would the Almighty really need to worry about his "street cred"? Could he be worried about losing face? Would that give his imagined enemies some advantage over him? It is absurd. What could threaten him? Why should he feel the insecurity that causes petty tyrants to inflict reprisals on those who badmouth them?

Ingersoll may be the only one who has noticed the problem:

> Various reasons are given for punishing the wicked: first, that God will vindicate his injured majesty. Well, I am glad of that! . . . I say here to-night that you cannot commit a sin against an infinite being. I can sin against my brother or my neighbour, because I can injure them. There can be no sin where there is no injury. Neither can a finite being commit infinite sin.[5]

Listen also to Alfred North Whitehead:

> As for the Christian theology, can you imagine anything more appallingly idiotic than the Christian idea of heaven? What kind of deity is it that would be capable of creating angels and men to sing his praises day and night to all eternity? It is, of course, the figure of an Oriental despot, with his inane and barbaric vanity. Such a conception is an insult to God.[14]

It's Who You Know

About that uncontacted Amazonian tribesman

On and on it goes. We have to ask why *belief* in God's plan of salvation would be necessary at all. If God, through Christ's death, has saved you by blotting out your sins, why do you have to *know* about it? Consider the logic of "Jesus died for the sins of mankind." What, *didn't it work?*

If the atonement doesn't work until and unless you acknowledge it in faith, then you'd have to say Jesus merely made it *possible* to be saved. Like Jonas Salk, he would seem to be the inventor of a vaccine, but you'd have to stand in line to get your sugar cube with the medicine in it. If you don't, you're still not "saved" from getting Polio.

That somehow seems inadequate, given all the Christian talk about Jesus simply "saving" us. Did he just make it *possible* for us to save ourselves? If Jesus saved us by his sacrifice, why would we be required to believe in it, and to affirm the truth of it? Many people have been rescued by some hidden benefactor without ever being aware of it.

You have probably heard devout Christians speculate over the ultimate fate of foreign people who dwell far beyond the reach of missionaries. They live and die without ever knowing about Jesus and the gospel of salvation. No one can bring himself to believe that these poor souls are automatically consigned to hell (though missionary fundraising rhetoric sometimes implies it). Sometimes the puzzled pious speculate that perhaps God saves or damns these heathens depending upon how well they live up to "the light they have." Did they strive to obey their consciences? God knows their hearts.

But in that case, shouldn't Christian missionaries just stay home? Are they doing the heathen any favors by setting new hurdles in their path? As soon as they blaze a trail through the jungle and tell "the good news," the natives are put in a much tighter spot, now being required to accept alien, improbable beliefs about unverifiable "realities." Weren't they better off before?

The same question comes up with the righteous people of the Old Testament. Even if they expected the eventual advent of a messianic king to restore the fortunes of Israel, there is just no way they could have looked forward to a divine Savior, an incarnation of God, who would sacrifice himself to expiate the sins of the world. That is Christian dogma pure and simple, so it cannot predate the Christian religion. And yet certainly the Old Testament heroes of the faith cannot have been sent to Gehenna for lack of clairvoyant knowledge of the Christian faith. Nobody thinks they were.

But, once again, if it was good enough for them to be faithful to what (little) they knew of God, why muddy the water by introducing a whole checklist of new beliefs that will be required for salvation from now on? Would such new doctrines be easy to accept? Look at the overwhelmingly negative reaction of Jews, ancient and modern, to Christian beliefs. Naturally. What else would you expect?

If pre-Christian Israelites got along just fine without knowing about Jesus and his cross, why can't the rest of us? This problem is so serious that some have resorted to a desperate expedient, suggesting (really, *pretending*) that everybody in ancient Israel *did* know all about Jesus and his eventual sacrifice. Calvinists (and Mormons) think the ancients would have read Isaiah chapter 53 ("He was wounded for our transgressions, he was bruised for our iniquities; upon him was the chastisement that made us whole, and with his stripes we are healed.") and recognized it as a prediction of Jesus on the cross. That is ludicrous, but these Christian apologists, assuming that the ancients read scripture through deep-dyed Christian lenses, feel forced to make such a maneuver.

Take a step back from this and ask yourself if one needs such Rube Goldberg-style *ad hoc* hypotheses to defend the plain truth. Doesn't such tortured rationalization mark the whole business as man-made fiction?

So why does Jesus demand belief in him, that he is the Christ or the Son of God or whatever? There's no inherent need for it. And that underlines the arbitrary nature of the whole thing. Socrates admonished his disciples, "Think not of Socrates, but think of the truth." [6] By contrast, Jesus insists that "I am the truth" (John 14:6), which is to ride the coattails of the truth and to claim for oneself the honor that is uniquely due the truth. He could have said, "I *speak* the truth," but that would have pointed away from himself to something that would be true no matter who said it.

As it is, pledging allegiance to Jesus is a forced loyalty oath, the kind required by those who know they do not deserve loyalty. Does Jesus deserve the allegiance a billion Christians pledge to him if he has to threaten them with eternal damnation to get it?

Jehovah, despite his murders, rapes, genocides, and pillaging, was content to let people alone after he killed them. It was left for Jesus to introduce the most unimaginable punishment of all: an eternity thrashing in a lake of fire, hopping about, shrieking, on the griddles of hell.

Mixed Signals

The contrast between Jesus and Jehovah turns out to be quite different from what first appeared. Jesus is by no means kinder and gentler than his Old Testament counterpart. In fact he is much more cruel!

But the real contradiction is between the opposing tendencies in Jesus' own teaching. James 3:11-12 takes it as self-evident common sense that fresh and brackish water cannot both issue from the same fountain. Yet in Jesus' teaching, they do. The result is incoherence, a seething mess of oxymoron.

Let's see if we can get this straight: God is like a human father, only better: more generous, more protective, more devoted. But he plans on putting to torture by far most of his creatures in eternal fire. The latter is simply unthinkable in view of the former, isn't it? A circle is not a square, and we cannot pretend it is even if God should tell us so. We will be pretending to believe what we know is not true and so destroying our integrity.

Some would rather admit the result is nonsense, covering their butt (and God's) with a euphemism: "I guess it's just a divine mystery, my son." But what good does *that* do you? Go ahead and quote Isaiah 55:9: "For as the heavens are higher than the earth, so are my ways higher than your ways and my thoughts than your thoughts." Nice try, but Jesus has said all too clearly that God is in fact closely analogous to good human fathers. And good fathers don't torture their children.

Besides, such a "mystery" tells us nothing. If we try to hybridize the "tender fatherhood" teaching with the "eternal hell" teaching, to split the difference, we vitiate both. It becomes a meaningless mix of oil and water. The obedient (obsequious?) Christian does not know what to believe anymore. And that is because there is no longer anything *to* believe. It's like saying, "Hey look! It's raining right outside the window. And it's *not* raining!" Uh, what's being asserted here? Nothing. It doesn't even rise to being false. It's just gibberish. And so is the gospel message of the tender master of hell-fire.

Some find the cognitive dissonance (the headache one gets from juggling incompatible beliefs) just too great. They try to resolve it by reinterpreting the hell passages, as some recent popes have done. Evangelical theologians, too, are eager to mitigate the doctrine of hell and damnation. A common move at this point is to suggest that Jesus and the Bible writers did not, heaven forbid, mean to tell us there is some literal lake or furnace of fire awaiting unrepentant unbelievers. Perish the thought! No, what Jesus "really" meant was that, when the sinners wake up dead, they will find themselves not sitting amid the flames like the Rich Man, but rather weeping in anguish over having missed their opportunity to bask forever in the beatific vision of God. "How could I have been such a fool!" Bummed out through endless ages.

But wait a second: Aren't we talking about people who were never interested in fellowship with God to begin with? Why would death change that? Wouldn't it be more consistent to picture these sinners partying it up forever with their impious pals?

Here's the absurd irony of this spin-doctoring revisionism: It implies that sinners, once they are dead, suddenly for the first time find themselves longing for God! In short, they have been *sanctified*, albeit too late! And despite themselves!

John Wesley once quipped that there is nothing sanctifying about the headsman's axe.[15] But I guess there is! We'd have to picture God sanctifying the sinners just to increase their torment, like Tantalus, forever denied the fulfillment of their desire—in this case, their brand new desire for God himself! That's like spurning a suitor and giving him the goodbye gift of a love potion.

But maybe there's a good idea here after all! If God is going to impose hell on sinners against their will, why doesn't he just *sanctify* them against their will? Make them snap out of it and love him, and then welcome these prodigals back home?

It makes plenty of sense to me, but then what gives me the right to revise and rewrite Christian theology? If you think you have the right to revise it, then you have to admit mere human beings cooked it up to begin with.

Some sophisticated theologians ask us to believe that the offensive bits of Jesus' teaching were the result of the limitation imposed by the incarnation. He couldn't see past all the assumptions of his culture while he was a part of it. But this is theologically fatal. How can we tell what elements of Jesus' teaching are culturally relative assumptions and which are genuine revelations from heaven? I can see no way. Can you?

Others take a different approach, though it ends up coming to the same thing. The reasoning runs like this: If we can recognize clear contradictions between sayings ascribed to Jesus in the gospels, a good explanation would be that he didn't say the aberrant ones. Maybe early Christians tried to put their own opinions into Jesus' mouth to lend them added clout. "I don't buy that! Oh, what's that? You say Jesus said it? Well, in that case . . ."

This is the approach of critical New Testament scholars including the Jesus Seminar, who try to isolate authentic sayings of

Jesus from spurious ones. But this, too, undermines and destroys any theological authority for either Jesus or the Bible, and that is why conservatives have so completely repudiated it. If it is up to me to decide what Jesus said and what he didn't (especially if these judgment calls are based on what sounds good to *me*), then *I* have become the authority, not Jesus, not scripture. I wind up saying, "I said it! Jesus believed it! That settles it!"

Notes

1. Robert Green Ingersoll, *Lecture on Hell.*

2. *Lecture on Hell.*

3. *Lecture on Hell.*

4. *Lecture on Hell.*

5. *Lecture on Hell.*

6. Plato, *Phaedo.*

7. Peter   Kingsley, *Ancient   Philosophy,   Mystery,   and   Magic: Empedocles and Pythagorean Tradition* (NY: Oxford University Press, 1995), pp. 86-87, 193.

8. George M. Lamsa, *Gospel Light: Comments from the Aramaic and Unchanged   Eastern   Customs   on   the   Teachings   of   Jesus* (Philadelphia: A.J. Holman, 1939), pp. 35-37.

9. Of course he would not have been commenting on a Christian gospel, but only on the meaning of "Gehenna."

10. George Eldon Ladd, "The Parable of the Sheep and the Goats in Recent Interpretation." In R.N. Longenecker, ed., *New Dimensions in New Testament Study* (Grand Rapids: Zondervan, 1974), pp. 197-198.

11. Rudolf Bultmann, *Jesus Christ and Mythology* (New York: Scribner's, 1958), p. 84.

12. Most early manuscripts lack Mark 16:16, but I include it anyway, since I am concerned here to treat the Bible the way Christian readers do. Fundamentalists have always been suspicious of textual criticism, the attempt to weed out interpolations added to the text of scripture over the centuries, because the bedrock of their faith is the Bible they have inherited and read from childhood. This explains the absurd notion one sometimes hears from the uneducated pious: "If the King

James Bible was good enough for Jesus, it's good enough for me!" They can see that starting to "tamper" with the scripture they got their faith from, that was read in their congregation, sets forth a process of erosion that may never end. Then they will never be able to rest confident that their faith is guaranteed by "the Bible" they know.

13. Bruce J. Malina, *The New Testament World: Insights from Cultural Anthropology* (Atlanta: John Knox Press, 1981), Chapter 2, "Honor and Shame: Pivotal Values of the First-Century Mediterranean World," pp. 25-50.

14. Lucien Price, *Dialogues of Alfred North Whitehead* (Boston: Little, Brown and Company, 1954), p. 277.

15. I think it was Wesley. In any case, I'm paraphrasing. The context of the statement was that the Christian is supposed to enter God's heavenly Presence perfectly sanctified. Unlike Roman Catholics, Protestants reject the notion of a Purgatory in which the purifying fires will "take up the slack" between earthly Christian mediocrity and heavenly perfection. And if *that's* not an option, how *do* you make the transition? There's no particular reason to imagine the mere fact of dying is going to close the gap, so what's the alternative? At least theoretically, it must be assumed that the Christian will get fully sanctified on this side of the grave, and there's no real reason he shouldn't.

V

No Escape

> If the cross was needed to pay the punishment for my sins, then how can God really be a forgiving God? Forgiveness doesn't require punishment. To put it bluntly, if I can't forgive you for striking me on the chin until I return the blow back to you, or to someone else, then that's not forgiveness—that's retaliation, or sweet revenge!
>
> —John W. Loftus,
> *Why I Became an Atheist*

"Can two walk together, except they be agreed?" (Amos 3:3 KJV). "What partnership have righteousness and iniquity? Or what fellowship has light with darkness? What accord has Christ with Belial?" (2 Cor. 6:14-15). You can't mix fire and water; the fire will evaporate the water or the water will extinguish the fire. Something can never be its opposite.

Who would deny this? Nor dare we deny the same truth when it comes to the Bible and Christian theology. Repeated acts of horror cannot be squared with the universally understood meaning of the words "love," "justice," "forgiveness" and "mercy." If we do not recognize these as irreconcilable opposites, we must deny that words have any meaning.

A creed that attempts to meld them together degenerates into speaking in tongues. You may feel very pious repeating such a creed, but you cannot mean anything by it. To be told that the same changeless deity taught the enlightened sentiments of the Sermon on the Mount *and* introduced the doctrine of everlasting torment creates intellectual schizophrenia in those who try to believe both.

We are told that "God is not the author of confusion" (1 Cor. 14:33). Indeed he cannot be, without being some kind of malevolent chaos dragon. So what kind of "revelation" is it that leaves its recipients more baffled than before? [2]

Ask yourself: Is the slate of drastic contradictions at fundamental points of the Bible—both those we've seen here and a bunch of others well known—more naturally explained as a revelation from God, contained in an infallible scripture inspired by God? Or as an almost random collection of fallible, altogether human, opinions?

For a devoted Christian believer, it is very difficult to accept the latter understanding. In doing so, you give up a great deal of accustomed comfort. You forfeit a solid sense of life's mission and meaning, of calling and direction. Of exemption from the fear of death.

On the other hand, such a realization relieves you of the chronic migraines of cognitive dissonance, of suppressing your doubts, of fearing to incur the displeasure of a God whose chastisements are imagined behind every daily misfortune. The yoke of Christ turns out not to be so easy, his burden not so light after all.

But if we cast it off our aching shoulders, we need no longer see the crimes of the Creator as instances of his justice. Let us consider some of them, reconsider others, in light of the possibility that they are just fictions hatched by the imaginations of ancients whose thoughts reflect a more savage time.

Cruel Creation

It is amazing how theologians tell us that God, having created us, has every right to do with us as he wishes, *and* that it is the fact of our creation by God that guarantees the rights and dignity of man. *What* rights? What *dignity*, if we are mere vessels fashioned by God for whatever use he may see fit, whether a chalice or a spittoon (Rom. 9:19-25; 2 Tim. 2:20)? These lines from A.E. Houseman aptly describe our predicament as creations of God: "I, a stranger and afraid in a world I never made."

Consider our position. We never asked to enter the world. Not that life is necessarily something to bemoan, but, given the Christian worldview, it does look like a raw deal. We are born as rats assigned to a maze. We end up before twin doors behind which wait the lady and the tiger: salvation and damnation. We are told we must choose, and we will be blamed for blundering into the hungry jaws of the tiger. And this despite the fact we were never given sufficient clues for making the right choice, like students tested on material never covered in class.

Think about the moral behavior of a God who threatens us with eternal damnation for reaching the wrong conclusion (deciding that, say, Buddhism, not Christianity, is true, or that the Trinity doctrine is false) while neglecting to provide sufficient evidence for us to determine the truth. He's made our eternal salvation nothing more than a mere game of chance! Are God and Satan placing bets on human guinea pigs again, like in the Book of Job?

The whole stable of human religions would seem to be running some gigantic horse race, with incredibly high stakes. For any one of them to win (assuming you buy at least one of their exclusivity claims), everybody else has to lose.

And that's not even factoring in God's perfect foreknowledge, which means the race is fixed. Like professional wrestling, the outcome is pre-determined, and it's just a spectacle for purposes of entertainment. It's not even an honest game of chance.

You have to envision God as scripting a movie where most of the characters are cast as part of the body count at the end. Calvinists have gone so far (though they often try to hide it with theological doubletalk) as to teach that God actually predestined (or at the very least, engineered) the Fall of man because he had this terrific "plan of salvation" in mind and, heck, he'd have no opportunity to use it unless people needed to be saved from something! As Ethan Allen once said, the whole business "has too much the appearance of human craft."[3]

Why would God do all this? Why create the mortal race just to serve as kindling for the fiery furnace of hell? And if he did want to do that, why the cat-and-mouse game? Just pull the trigger and get it over with, for Pete's sake.

Isn't it obvious by now that theologians have tied themselves (and their hapless Christian followers) in knots trying to make fragments of ancient myth into a rational system? They are so deep into it, so deeply invested in it, that they cannot recognize how much they've reduced their own belief to absurdity.

There has to come a point when you take a look around and realize you've gone way off the track someplace. And then you'd better retrace your steps. That's what I'm asking you to do in this book.

That Appalling Apple

Let's narrow our focus to a particular, and pivotal, case of bungled theological reverse-engineering: Adam and Eve and the Fall of humanity. The Garden of Eden story is often said to be symbolically rich, susceptible to multiple interpretations. This is a euphemistic way of saying that it is not at all clear what the story is supposed to mean.

The most familiar reading of the tale (Gen. 2-3) interprets it as recording the cataclysmic ruination of humanity by way of eating the forbidden fruit. God told them to keep their hands off a certain type of fruit, just as an arbitrarily chosen test of obedience. There's nothing important about the fruit, just the act. The first couple failed the test, preferring the hissing counsel of a talking snake, who was, to use Elvis's famous phrase, "the devil in disguise." This breach of trust alienated God and man, corrupting human nature and incurring the Creator's wrath toward not only Adam and Eve but all their future progeny as well, including you and me.

The story and this "orthodox" interpretation of it are beset with difficulties both logical and scientific. One of them is the question of how Adam and Eve, innocents in Eden, could be judged guilty of wrongdoing when they knew nothing yet about good and evil.[4]

If it already had been evil to do what they did, doesn't that mean they *already* harbored the deadly germ of sin? What changed with their act? This seems to be a pretty big clue that the traditional

Christian reading has got the story wrong. Interestingly, Judaism does not understand this story as accounting for the origin of evil. Accordingly, Jews do not believe in Original Sin.

Instead, they believe that God gives two rival inclinations to every individual: the evil imagination and the good imagination.[5] It's just like the cartoons depicting someone considering a moral dilemma; a miniature devil sits on one shoulder while a tiny angel perches on the other, each making his case to the tempted man. It is always an open option. The outcome is not pre-decided.

When one opts for sin, Judaism teaches, one can count on God's forgiveness if and when one sincerely repents. That's all it takes. (Yes, I know there were elaborate sacrifices of animals and produce, but these were a kind of "religious sterilization" protocol to remove "ritual defilement" or "ceremonial uncleanness," a very different matter–see below).

So where did Christians get the doctrine of Original Sin, an all-pervasive perversion of human nature, coupled with second-hand guilt for "those whose sin was not like Adam's" (Rom. 5:14)? The whole human race, untold billions of people, all descended from Adam, born condemned for what he and Eve did, despite not even existing while the first parents were dwelling in the Secret Garden. How did such an outlandish idea ever get established?

It is a matter of reverse engineering. Early Christians had to deal with the death of Jesus somehow. He was executed as a criminal, but they believed he wasn't one. So if he didn't die for any sins of his own, and his death couldn't have been a meaningless tragedy, whose sins *did* he die for? Must have been *everybody else's*!

But wait a second! Couldn't God have simply *forgiven* everybody their sins? Either with a declaration of universal amnesty or a case-by-case absolution any time a sinner sought forgiveness? Well, of course, but that was already true, right? Jesus or no Jesus. So, to justify Jesus' death as necessary for salvation, Christians figured there must have been some sort of deeper problem, some spiritual cancer, a congenital curse, that required radical surgery: something more metaphysical than moral. Call it "Original Sin." Sure! That ought to do it! Otherwise "Christ died to no purpose" (Gal. 2:21).

But, oh what a mockery of elementary justice this creates! Pioneer patriot Ethan Allen saw the connecting link between the two basic moral confusions in Eden and Calvary. Both presuppose *the imputation of sin*. That is, assigning blame to those who did not incur it. We descendants of Adam and Eve have surely committed some bad acts of our own, but we're really up the creek because of Adam and Eve. It's like somebody discovering that all his deceased parents bequeathed him was a pile of debts that *he* must pay. Thanks a lot! Even some writers of the Bible see the injustice here.

> The soul that sins shall die. The son shall not suffer for the iniquity of the father, nor the father suffer for the iniquity of the son; the righteousness of the righteous shall be upon himself, and the wickedness of the wicked shall be upon himself. (Ezek. 18:20)

> In those days they shall no longer say: "The fathers have eaten sour grapes, and the children's teeth are set on edge." But every one shall die for his own sin; each man who eats sour grapes, his teeth shall be set on edge. (Jer. 31:29-30)

On the other hand, how does it comport with any possible definition of justice for God to let sinners off the hook by piling their guilt on the back of an innocent man? Even if that man is willing to volunteer as the scapegoat, why does that change anything? Hosea Ballou[6] posed this analogy: Imagine the President's security men nabbing a would-be assassin. He is slated for execution. But then the President takes pity on his nemesis and volunteers to be executed in his place! Granted, that might be pretty nice of him, but would that make it just? It's not like paying your buddy's traffic ticket for him.[7]

Ethan Allen was debating a Calvinist and pointing out the unfairness of God imputing Adam's sins to the rest of us. But then his opponent replied (and I'm paraphrasing), "Then what do you think was going on at Calvary? Wasn't God imputing your sin to Jesus Christ? That's how he saved you!" And Allen realized he was right! The one was just as morally nonsensical as the other! From that day on, Ethan Allen was a Deist.[8]

Password to Paradise

Is it bigotry to insist that one can be saved only through pledging allegiance to Jesus? Defenders of the faith have a point: It wouldn't *have* to be. After all, is it bigoted for a doctor to tell you that drinking Seven-Up is not going to cure your cancer? Go ahead and believe it if you want to, but it's just not true. And it's not going to save you. That's a fact. And the doctor's not a bigot for telling you so.

Not all opinions, however cherished, are equally true. Is there any way to test whether Socialism or Capitalism is the road to prosperity? I should say that there is. Put each into practice and examine the results. In short, if you have good reasons for confidence in this proposed solution or that hypothesis, it cannot be called bigotry to champion it over against other options. Even if you turn out to be mistaken, you still weren't a bigot.

Applied to the exclusivity of the Christian salvation doctrine, this means that you would certainly not be a bigot to sport one of those lapel badges some of us used to wear proudly back in the early 1970s, which featured a hand with the index finger pointing skyward with the slogan "One Way!" If, that is, you had good reasons to think so. But do you? Really?

I used to think so, until I had to admit I was merely looking for clever arguments to back up what I wanted to believe. Once again, it is reverse-engineering, rationalizing, working backwards from a desired "conclusion." It's not really a conclusion if it's what you started out with!

For many centuries, Christian believers figured they had pretty impressive reasons for believing that "there is no other name under heaven, given among men, whereby we must be saved" (Acts 4:12).

What were these sure-fire credentials? Number one was the force of all those biblical miracles, especially the ones ascribed to Jesus in the gospels. Anyone who could turn water into wine, walk on water, multiply bread and fish, cleanse lepers, restore the deaf and the blind, and even rise from the dead after his own execution—well, who could he be other than God on earth, or the Son of God?

It all sounds pretty impressive until you realize that we don't really *have* any miracles, as if we ourselves had seen them. All we have is a batch of *stories* about miracles. And two thousand years separate us from these ostensible miracles. Who knows where the stories may ultimately have come from?

Apologists [9] like to argue at this point that there is this, that, and the other reason to believe that the stories were written down by eye-witnesses, or at least by people who had heard it from front-line reporters, however many steps back. And why would those people have lied about it? Wouldn't they have been exposed as liars by hostile witnesses?

Those repeating these arguments—fragile, tortuous, and hypothetical as they are—never seem to notice that they are *themselves* factors that undermine and dilute our confidence in these old tales. The tendency of all such reasonings is, at most, to show there is a way to show that, conceivably, the stories *might possibly* have come from authoritative testimony. But mere possibility is far from probability or even from plausibility.

The author of the Gospel of John seems to have uneasily realized this and tried to compensate. John 20 has Thomas absent when the resurrected Jesus magically appears out of nowhere to the flabbergasted disciples. Given that the purpose of the visit is to impart the Holy Spirit to the apostles and thus equip them for their future mission (John 20:21-23), you'd think the supernatural Christ might have waited till everybody was present. But no.

"Hey, where's Tom? Gee, I'm sorry I missed him!" one can imagine him saying, then completing his business and popping back into the ether. Thomas returns from some errand and hears the news.

"Sorry, guys," he says, "I'm going to have to have more than your say-so before I'll believe *that* one!" A few days later, Jesus returns to convince Thomas with a special command performance. Like Job cowed by the epiphany of God in the cyclone, Thomas bows and wishes he hadn't been such a smart aleck.

Jesus reassures him, "Have you believed because you have seen me? Blessed are those who have not seen and yet believe" (John 20:29).

Lucky Tom! He is a fictional stand-in for all Christians who have nothing but holy hearsay to go on. Like us, he finds that an insufficient basis to believe a whopper like the resurrection of Jesus. And he gets what *we* would like to get, what we *need* to get: direct proof. We readers are supposed to be mollified by that? We are not supposed to notice that it, too, is just one more story among the rest.

Some like to point to the quick success of the Christian gospel (though sociologists [10] show the early Christian growth rate is by no means more impressive than that of analogous sects like the Mormons or the Unification Church of Sun Myung Moon) as somehow proving the divine origin of Christianity. Christians argue that the faith could never have spread so far so fast without some pretty compelling evidence to back up their claims. The early evangelists' preaching of the resurrected Christ must have been pretty convincing!

Well, it *might* have been—if only we knew what they said! Again we are being asked to believe simply on the basis that someone else did! What's conspicuously absent is any convincing miracle or revelation made to us *today*, when it counts. If the doubters two millennia ago required such proof and received it, why shouldn't we need it, and receive it, too? [11]

Why should we be blamed for our "lack of faith"? Is there some virtue to being gullible? Is gullibility the real criterion for salvation? Is that what they mean by "faith"? I should say that one is to be blamed, not for rejecting such summonses to believe without evidence, but for accepting them.

There is one more Bible passage which I think is every bit as apropos to this whole question as is Acts 4:12 ("there is no other name under heaven, given among men, whereby we must be saved"), and that is Judges 12:5-7:

> And the Gileadites took the fords of the Jordan against the Ephraimites. And when any of the fugitives of Ephraim said, "Let me go over," the men of Gilead said to him, "Are you an Ephraimite?" When he said, "No," they said to him, "Then say Shibboleth," and he said, "Sibboleth," for he could not pronounce it right; then they seized him and slew him at the fords of the Jordan. And there fell at that time forty-two thousand of the Ephraimites.

For us, the world *shibboleth* has come to denote "litmus test," some opinion that qualifies one as a true Republican, Marxist, whatever. But originally it meant simply a password, as arbitrary as the correct pronunciation of a foreign word. And I am suggesting that, in the absence of adequate evidence, to confess the name of Jesus is fully as arbitrary as getting "shibboleth" right. And so is the imagined penalty (at God's hands) for getting it wrong.

So is it bigotry to demand confession of Jesus Christ as the password to salvation? Yes, it is. All the fancy theology once more turns out to be a rationale for intolerance and scare tactics.

A Sin That Will Live in Infamy

We have already discussed the vast incongruity between a sin, *any* sin, committed by ephemeral non-entities like us, and the surpassing vastness of the Absolute, the Infinite, the Eternal. Can anything we do have such vast ripples in the cosmic ocean? It makes sense only on the basis of assumptions that make even *less* sense: those of feudal justice. But there is more.

There is the venerable doctrine of divine *aseity*. The word derives from the Latin *a se*, "from itself." What this means is that God is self-contained in the sense of being unconditioned, unaffected by any influences, invulnerable to all harm from anything a creature may do.

Can you hurt God physically? Obviously not, for he is not limited to physical form. Can you hurt him emotionally by, say, rejecting his love or defying his will? You may do these things, but God is not injured by them. Otherwise, we puny motes should wield power over the Almighty, as we do over each other when one person's rejection breaks another's heart. Of course scripture often speaks of God's wrath against sin, or his disappointment and grief over the unrepentant, but theologians tell us that, since God *cannot* be so affected, then he *isn't* so affected. Such language is all just metaphor—for a vague something at which hands are piously waved.

Fine. But doesn't this sublime invincibility rule out any possibility of God's honor or majesty being injured? Does not the very idea of God becoming riled or shamed by the impotent blasphemies of insignificant human ants become laughable? Not that he feels it, but the very idea is *itself* demeaning to God.

And if this is so, then all basis for ascribing infinite gravity, and infinite penalty, to any human sin vanishes away. We have to call it one more instance of theological sleight-of-hand, a childish scare story to frighten the superstitious into cowed obedience to self-appointed religious "authorities."

Cross Purposes
The bizarre idea of blood sacrifice

Are not things topsy-turvy when Christians contemplate the violent death of Jesus on the Cross of Calvary and tearfully call it the greatest monument of God's mercy? In fact, the gorier they imagine it (as in Mel Gibson's film *The Passion of the Christ*), the more they weep with tender gratitude.

I have already tried to show how completely alien to any notion of justice (if the word is to mean anything) is the idea of the crucifixion as an atonement for sin. But there is another issue, equally baffling. And that is the "mechanics" of the atonement. *How* are we to imagine the execution of Jesus as a remedy for sin, a means of restoring intimacy between God and the human race? What on earth can the one have to do with the other?

The New Testament sometimes refers to Christ's death as an *expiation* for sin (1 John 4:10). This model of salvation is frequently confused with the one we have already rejected, *penal substitution*. That makes the crucified Jesus into a kind of whipping boy, taking the punishment for wrongs done by others, a gross parody of justice. But expiation belongs to an altogether different frame of reference. It is a technical term stemming from the ancient sacrificial system of Israel. There were very many acts, often necessary to daily life, that rendered one "unclean" before God.

One could not appear before God in the temple while in an unclean condition. Touching a running wound (or someone who had one) rendered one unclean, but no one thought a physician immoral for having done so. It wasn't remotely a question of morality. Menstruating women were temporarily rendered unclean, but no one blamed them for it. Childbirth made a woman ritually impure, but this hardly meant you were to avoid having children. Touching corpses made you unclean, but burying the dead was a crucial responsibility as well as a prime act of charity toward the indigent.

Depending on what had rendered you ritually unclean, there were various remedies, "purifications." They ranged from just waiting till sundown to taking a bath to offering an animal sacrifice. If you sacrificed an animal, you'd place your hand on its head as a priest slit its throat. The gushing blood would flow over you, and this washed away your ritual impurity. It expiated your sin.

That whole conceptuality is alien to us. But nowadays we are to believe that we are saved by being "washed in the blood of the Lamb." Really?

You can't simply pluck this one feature out of a conceptual

framework that no longer makes sense to us. It only seems to fit into a Christian theological context because people blur it together with penal substitution, as if they meant the same thing. But the imagery does survive, however ghastly and grotesque it strikes modern ears, as in a well-known hymn that says,

There is a fountain filled with blood
   drawn from Emmanuel's veins;
   and sinners plunged beneath that flood
   lose all their guilty stains.[1]

It is just plain amazing that any devout Christian can find this edifying.

Jesus is called *the Redeemer*, and this refers to yet another model of salvation, *redemption* or *ransom*. These parallel metaphors (if that's all they are) envision the death of Jesus as the price of liberating the human race from bondage. "Redemption" (Gal. 3:13; Rev. 14:3-4) implies that God is buying the freedom of slaves. "Ransom" (Matt. 20:28; Mark 10:45; 1 Tim. 2:6; 1 Pet. 1:18; Rev. 5:9) implies that the death of Jesus is a price paid to kidnappers holding the human race hostage.

The inevitable question: Who was the slave owner? Who was the kidnapper? The answer drags the atonement doctrine into the realm of raw myth.

The classical understanding of this version of the atonement, going back to the fourth century, pictures Satan as the one in possession of a sinful humanity. It is the devil with whom God must negotiate in order to save us, using his Son as a bargaining chip.

You see, humanity had mortgaged itself to the Prince of Darkness by succumbing to sin. Now he had them where he wanted them. And God wanted them back! But Satan refused to let them go free unless he was compensated. So God offered the soul of his Son in return for Old Scratch's whole butterfly collection of souls.[12] But the devil got snookered, little expecting Jesus to rise from the dead no sooner than he arrived on hell's doorstep, leaving Satan holding the bag! Let me just observe that, if the goal is to make some sense of the doctrine of the cross, this may not be the way to go. The cure would seem to be worse than the disease.

More liberal-leaning Christians sometimes gravitate to the *moral influence* theory of the atonement. Romans 5:8 and 1 John 3:16; 4:9-10 both suggest that the cross was the pre-eminent token of God's love for us. But how so? How does the brutal execution of God's Son demonstrate, even suggest, that God loves mankind? This theory was designed to retire all the previous, rather bizarre, theories of the cross in favor of saying that the cross simply, somehow, woos us, wins us over, by showing us the full extent of God's love. But does this hold water?

———

Let's consider an example that shows the difference between a real demonstration of love and an act of self-harm that accomplishes nothing. Suppose you and I are about to cross the street. We are chatting, and out of the corner of my eye I catch sight of an out-of-control bus hurtling toward us. You have stepped out just ahead of me, oblivious of the danger you're in. In a split second I realize I have only a single choice. I throw myself against you, knocking you aside but landing in the path of the rogue vehicle myself! I get hit and crushed by the bus.

Amid the bloody chaos, you look at my remains and gasp, "He gave his life for me! I never knew how much he loved me!"

But suppose I notice a bus approaching at a normal clip, even beginning to slow down to discharge passengers. I say to you, "Watch this!" And I dive into the path of the bus, gratuitously ending my own life.

You are left in baffled horror. "My God! He must have been insane! I never suspected!"

You see the difference, right? In the first instance, my death was a heroic sacrifice, demonstrating my love for you because my death was the concrete means of rescuing you. "Greater love has no man than this, that a man lay down his life for his friends" (John 15:13). Of course!

But in the second instance, the gratuitous spectacle of my suicide communicates absolutely nothing of love or sacrifice. The moral influence theory of the atonement is like the second scenario: it conspicuously lacks any link between the death and love. My death benefits no one. Only if *in some specific way* it secures your well-being does it also spell love.

And this fatal flaw, though a bit less obviously, vitiates the other theories, too. Even if these theological "explanations" are implausibly far-fetched, they do at least try to explain what Jesus accomplished by his death. Thus they understand that it is the thing achieved on our behalf—liberation from Satan's captivity, purification of ceremonial stains by a bloodbath, switching places with the rightful occupant of the electric chair—and not the sheer fact of the death itself that demonstrates the love of God or Christ for us.

But the atonement is still not out of the woods as long as the specific link between Christ's death and our salvation makes no sense. "You can't get there from here."

———

So where are we? Just as in Mel Gibson's celluloid gospel, in which all the characters speak nothing but Aramaic, we see in the crucifixion nothing but sadistic, bloody violence with no intelligible explanation.

Notes

1. "There Is a Fountain Filled with Blood," United Methodist Hymnal No. 622, Text by William Cowper, 1731-1800.

2. Ethan Allen, *Reason the Only Oracle of Man, Or a Compendious System of Natural Religion* (Bennington, VT: Haswell & Russell, 1784), pp. 207, 227.

3. Allen, p. 340.

4. Allen, p. 364. In just the same way, in Exodus 32, Moses comes down from Mount Sinai only to be horrified that his people are committing

idolatry, an infraction of one of the commandments he was about to give them. In other words, he condemned them for breaking a command that hadn't even been issued yet!

5. Solomon   Schechter, *Some Aspects of Rabbinic Theology* (NY: Macmillan, 1910), Chapter XV. "The Evil Yezer: The Sources of Rebellion," pp. 242-263.

6. Hosea Ballou, *A Treatise on Atonement; In which the Finite Nature of Sin is Argued, its Cause and Consequences as Such; The Necessity and Nature of Atonement; and its Glorious Consequences, in the Final   Reconciliation of All Men to Holiness and Happiness* (Hallowell: C. Spaulding, Third ed., 1828), pp. 79-80.

7. Allen, pp. 414-415.

8. Allen, pp. 386-391.

9. John Warwick Montgomery, *History & Christianity* (Downers Grove, IL: InterVarsity Press, 1974); F.F. Bruce, *The   New Testament Documents: Are They Reliable?* (Grand Rapids: Eerdmans, 1972); J.N.D. Anderson, *Christianity: The Witness of History* (London: Tyndale Press, 1969); Michael Green, *Man Alive!* (Downers Grove, IL: Inter-Varsity Press, 1971); John R.W. Stott, *Basic Christianity* (Grand Rapids: Eerdmans, 1958).

10. Rodney Stark, *The Rise of Christianity: A Sociologist Reconsiders History* (Princeton: Princeton University Press, 1996), Chapter 1, "Conversion and Christian Growth," pp. 3-27.

11. Allen, pp. 262-263.

12. Think here of the parable of the Pearl of Great Price, where the pearl merchant is willing to cash in his entire stock in order to buy a giant, perfect pearl worth all the rest put together–Matthew 13:45-46.

VI

No sign of Jesus

> A skeptic could hardly ask for a more objective falsification of any religion: the religion's leader prophesies a globally identifiable series of events within a specified time period, but the events do not take place within that time period. Yet Christianity did not fail after the first generation; there were already too many believers with too much at stake, and when the fuzzy boundary of one generation was passed, reason was not going to stand in the way of the movement, since reason was not the primary impetus for Christians to believe in the first place.
>
> —Kenneth Daniels, *Why I Believed: Reflections of a Former Missionary*

The Missing Man

There is an ironic aptness to the gospel saying, "The Son of man is coming at an hour you do not expect" (Matt. 24:44). Put differently, and more clearly, Jesus Christ cannot be found where you have every right to expect him to be!

First, he has not returned to this earth by the deadline he himself clearly set. As we shall see below, Jesus explicitly said to his followers that they could expect his return within their lifetimes, and it didn't happen.

Second, there is no trace of any human historical Jesus in the epistles of Paul, which were penned before any of the gospels. This is inconceivable; one must imagine that the relevance of Jesus, as well as Christians' curiosity about him, would have been much more powerful at the beginning than now.

Wouldn't you expect that first-century Christians would have known (and discussed) much more of the teaching and life of their Savior than we do today? And those scattered throughout the Mediterranean world, not having been present to see and hear him for themselves (1 Pet. 1:8), would have pressed Jesus' apostles for far more information about him than ever gets mentioned in the epistles written to them. But, *nada*.

Third, if Jesus was anything at all like the superhero celebrated in the gospels, his absence from any contemporary literature, formal or informal, is absolutely bewildering. It's an argument from silence, but that silence is deafening.

You can see where I am going with this; these startling facts speak pretty loudly for themselves. And what they say is really damning to the gospel portrait of Jesus, even raising the serious question whether any Jesus Christ existed at all, though that is not really my point in this chapter.

No historical Jesus? Believe what you want about that, it doesn't matter for this discussion. But no *gospel* Jesus? That's a problem.

Jerusalem, We Have a Problem

The New Testament speaks of Christians, collectively, as betrothed to Christ (2 Cor. 11:2-3; Eph. 5:25-31; Rev. 19:7-8) and refers to the glorious Messianic Banquet as "the Marriage Supper of the Lamb" (Rev. 19:9). The trouble is that the groom left the bride standing at the altar, and for a very long time—some two thousand years ago.

Christians don't mind poking fun (to put it mildly) at Jehovah's Witnesses for setting a series of dates for the predicted Second Coming of Christ. It was scheduled for 1914, with no visible result. Several recalculations were no more accurate. The Millerites had already posited an ETA in 1843, a terrific embarrassment.

More recently, there have been a whole series of such misfires, few of them receiving much media attention until Calvinist radio host Harold Camping told his audience to get ready for Jesus to touch down in 1994. Oops! Back to the drawing board! A nationwide campaign by Camping's fans then proclaimed with great conviction that Jesus was due back before the end of 2011. They wound up, of course, as extremely unhappy Campers.

Let's face it: All these poor souls made jackasses of themselves. They proved, among other things, Santayana's dictum that those who refuse to learn the lessons of history are doomed to repeat them. But mainstream Christians, while shaking their heads at the follies of these sectarians, are suffering from a far more serious case of amnesia.

It never occurs to them that their own religion suffered the very same ghastly embarrassment at the very beginning. That's when their Christ predicted he would revisit the earth before the generation of his contemporaries had passed away. The gospels have him making this obviously failed prophecy not just once, but several times:

Mark 13 is called "the Little Apocalypse" or "the Olivet Discourse." In it Jesus alerts an inner circle of his disciples to what they can expect to see as history ticks its way to its appointed conclusion. There will be wars and rumors of war, plagues, famines, persecutions, astronomical catastrophes—all issuing in the grand appearance in the sky of the Son of Man, Jesus himself, who will judge the wicked and save the believers.

When? During *his generation.* "Truly, I say to you, this generation will not pass away before all these things take place" (Mark 13:30).

Mark 8:38-9:1, similarly, has Jesus say, "For whoever is ashamed of me and of my words in this adulterous and sinful generation, of him will the Son of man also be ashamed, when he comes in the glory of his Father with the holy angels." And, he added, "Truly, I say to you, there are some standing here who will not taste death before they see that the kingdom of God has come with power."

Matthew 10:23 is even more cringe-inducing. "When they persecute you in one town, flee to the next; for truly, I say to you, you will not have gone through all the towns of Israel before the Son of man comes."

If words mean anything, these passages all depict Jesus predicting his return well before the close of the first century A.D. Looked at the calendar lately?

Pooh-poohing the Parousia

Erasing an embarrassing prophecy

Attentive Christians have recognized that these passages contain a deadly threat to their faith. Jesus was like the Millerites, the Jehovah's Witnesses, and Harold Camping. He was wrong, wildly wrong. And how wrong is that?

Fundamentalists argue that we can be sure everything Jesus taught is true because his resurrection from the dead vindicated his claims to be a divine revealer. Of course, the trouble with such blustering is that the resurrection of Jesus is far from verifiable, really *impossible* to verify at this late date. You can't use as a trump card a "fact" that is itself highly debatable.

But consider the logic of their argument: Most everything Jesus said referred to ostensible "realities" that are invisible to mortal eyes. The only way to become convinced of such claims is by means of some confirmation that *is* visible and verifiable, in other words, a visible tip of an invisible iceberg. Fundamentalists think Easter provides that verification. But it doesn't. It's up for grabs, as endless books and debates make clear.

The resurrection is an *object* of faith, not the *basis* for faith. So what might be a suitable rock on which to build this house? Obviously, if Jesus should appear in the sky, mounted legions of sword-bearing angels in tow, that would pretty much vindicate the divine authority of Jesus and the truth of Christianity. There is an Old Testament version of this prospect, too, in Isaiah 2:2-4.

It shall come to pass in the latter days
   that the mountain of the house of the LORD
   shall be established as the highest of the mountains,
   and shall be raised above the hills;
   and all the nations shall flow to it,
   and many peoples shall come, and say:
      "Come, let us go up to the mountain of the LORD,
      to the house of the God of Jacob;
      that he may teach us his ways
      and that we may walk in his paths."

For out of Zion shall go forth the law,
and the word of the LORD from Jerusalem.

He shall judge between the nations,
and shall decide for many peoples;
and they shall beat their swords into plowshares,
and their spears into pruning hooks;
nation shall not lift up sword against nation,
neither shall they learn war any more.

In this predicted scenario, God has miraculously vindicated Israel and restored her sovereignty. Seeing that, the Gentiles will have no choice but to conclude that the Jews had been right and they, the heathens, had been wrong. It would now be pretty clear which God and which religion were true, and which were false. The nations would naturally line up for a crash course in Jehovah-worship.

Well, yes. If all the world's present Buddhists, Jews, Hindus, and atheists were to tune into Cable News and see the apocalyptic appearance of Jesus Christ above Mount Zion, there'd be a lot of hasty conversions! Such a sight would result in a whole lot of books and pamphlets by Robert G. Ingersoll, Richard Dawkins, and Bertrand Russell being relegated to the kindling basket.

But it didn't happen. Furthermore, there is no use in waiting for it still to happen. You see, Jesus did not say, "Someday, some century, some millennium, I plan to return." No, his promise included a statute of limitation: "*This generation* shall not pass away," and "There are *some standing here,*" and "You will not have finished going through the towns of Israel until . . ." Oy vey.

What about the corroboration factor? Remember, Jesus spoke of invisible things (cf. "we look not to the things that are seen but to the things that are unseen," 2 Cor. 4:18). For all we know, they might be true, but the deadline prediction of his apocalyptic Second Coming is the one thing he said that cannot remain among the unseen things. If this one is true, then "they will see the Son of man coming in clouds with great power and glory" (Mark 13:26).

There's just no avoiding this: The single necessary and sufficient guarantee of the truth of Jesus' doctrine failed. As Hermann Samuel Reimarus said, you can quote all the supposedly fulfilled prophecies you want, but that's not going to change the fact that Jesus didn't return on schedule.[1] Jesus' only falsifiable teaching has in fact *been* falsified. He was a first-century Harold Camping.

Such desperate predicaments prompt desperate measures. Defenders of the infallibility of scripture and the credibility of Jesus (which kind of end up being the same thing, Jesus being a creature of the Bible) have devoted considerable ingenuity to making an escape. But all of their proposals are so contrived and far-fetched that they would never look good to anyone who was not trying his best to get out of a tight spot.

Their efforts actually make matters worse for the stubborn believer, as we have seen in previous chapters. With transparently text-twisting arguments like the ones we will now consider—well, with defenses like these, who needs attacks?

I know this all too well from the pain of trying to "audition" these arguments long ago, in an attempt to salvage my own evangelical faith. Make of them what you will, but I cannot hide my very personal disappointment with them.

———

Starting with the Mark 13 "this generation will not pass away" prediction, is it possible that Jesus really meant "this *race*"? Well, the Greek word *genea* does sometimes mean that, but it cannot mean it in this context. The Jewish nation will not go extinct, or be wiped out, before the Second Coming of Christ? Such a theme is otherwise conspicuously absent from the rest of the discourse. If this is what Jesus meant, it is certainly odd that the question of Jewish survival should pop up here, out of nowhere, and just as quickly vanish.

On the other hand, the context makes it plain that Jesus is talking about a temporal timetable leading up to the end of the world. All these passages are from Mark:

- "This must take place, but the end is not yet" (13:7).

- "This is but the beginning of the sufferings" (13:8).

- "And the gospel must first be preached to all nations" (13:10).

- "If the Lord had not shortened the days, no human being would be saved; for the sake of the elect, whom he chose, he shortened the days" (13:20).

- "From the fig tree learn its lesson: as soon as the branch becomes tender and puts forth its leaves, you know that summer is near. So also, when you see these things taking place, you know that he is near, at the very gates" (13:29).

Thus *genea* really has to mean "this generation." [2]

A fall-back interpretation is that, though Jesus does mean "generation," he does not mean "this" generation as that of "some standing here," his contemporaries. Rather, he merely means that whatever generation happens to be alive at the time of these events will not die till they, er, do in fact see them. That's a tautology, like saying "A bachelor is a man who hasn't gotten married yet." It's absolutely pointless. Come on: Get real!

One school of "thought" suggests that there is no failed prediction here at all. What Jesus is predicting is simply the fall of Jerusalem to the Romans and the destruction of the Jerusalem temple in 70 A.D. Of course, that is one of the events on the table in Mark 13, but what about everybody seeing the descent of the Son of Man? It's, ah, just Technicolor symbolism. The end of the "world" just refers to the religious "world" of Judaism which, with the temple's destruction, is scheduled to give way to the Christian dispensation.

Do these "Preterists" (as they're called) [3] mean to say Christians have always been wrong to expect a literal return of Jesus? If they do, that's a pretty big price to pay. They are amputating a limb or two to save their patient.

But some say Jesus *did* return in person during the Roman siege of Jerusalem to rapture out the apostolic church, though in the attendant chaos nobody noticed. Uh . . . what about Revelation 1:7? "Behold, he is coming with the clouds, and every eye will see him, every one who pierced him; and all the tribes of the earth will wail on account of him"?

Dead Letters

Paul's awkward silence about Jesus

Just as ridiculous, and exposing just as clearly the man-made, patched-up character of the Christian faith, is the excuse-making necessitated by this astonishing fact: There is virtually nothing about the gospel Jesus in the Pauline epistles.

Really?, you ask. Nothing about an itinerant teacher or persecution and execution at the hands of Herodian and Roman officials? No quotations of Jesus even when they would certainly have solved various questions and problems Paul deals with in his writings? Yes, all true.

Some defenders of the faith try to throw their voice, reading the gospels into the epistles, in order to fill that silence. Why? Because they fear the implications.

Now, I realize that this is not an issue for your average pious Bible reader. For believers in biblical inspiration and infallibility, it makes no difference at all whether a command or a bit of revealed information is found in the Gospel of John, the Book of Proverbs, or the leaden 1 and 2 Chronicles. The Bible is the Bible. But conservative Bible *scholars* are forced to address the problem because, increasingly, doubters and skeptics throw it in their faces.

How about miracles? None of them, either—Paul mentions no healings, exorcisms, or anything else out of the ordinary done by Jesus, other than appearing to him "out of due time" (1 Cor. 15:8). Indeed, Paul practically says there weren't any miracles: "Jews demand signs and Greeks seek wisdom, but we preach Christ crucified, a stumbling block to Jews and folly to Gentiles" (1 Cor. 1:22-23).[4]

At least there is that "Roman cross," right? Well, if Paul thought Jesus was put to death by Roman and Jewish political authorities, it's hard to imagine him writing this:

> Let every person be subject to the governing authorities. For there is no authority except from God, and those that exist have been instituted by God. Therefore he who resists the authorities resists what God has appointed, and those who resist will incur judgment. For rulers are not a terror to good conduct, but to bad. Would you have no fear of him who is in authority? Then do what is good, and you will receive his approval, for he is God's servant for your good. But if you do wrong, be afraid, for he does not bear the sword in vain; he is the servant of God to execute his wrath on the wrongdoer. (Rom. 13:1-4) [5]

Granted, Paul says Jesus was done in by "the rulers of this age" (1 Cor. 1:2:6-8):

> Yet among the mature we do impart wisdom, although it is not a wisdom of this age or of the rulers of this age, who are doomed to pass away. But we impart a secret and hidden wisdom of God, which God decreed before the ages for our glorification. None of the rulers of this age understood this; for if they had, they would not have crucified the Lord of glory.

But the point here is that Christ was slain by the fallen angels [6] who figure prominently in apocalyptic Judaism and in Gnostic mysticism.[7] Colossians 2:13-15 says:

> And you, who were dead in trespasses and the uncircumcision of your flesh, God made alive together with him, having forgiven us all our trespasses, having canceled the bond which stood against us with its legal demands; this he set aside, nailing it to the cross. He disarmed the principalities and powers and made a public example of

them, triumphing over them in him.

These "principalities and powers" are, again, the fallen angels (or "sons of God" from Genesis 6:1-4). Paul is not talking about some judicial altercation involving earthly governments. The crucifixion he envisions is a celestial event like that described in Gnostic texts.

This sounds very alien, even absurd, to modern Christian ears, but that is because we have been taught that Paul was well aware of the gospels' crucifixion accounts with Pilate and Herod, and that he must have been referring to them.[8] We can dismiss the mention of Pilate in 1 Timothy 6:13 by noting that both epistles "to Timothy" (along with Titus) were much later works written in Paul's name by some latter-day admirer, which is acknowledged by virtually all scholars who are not party-line fundamentalists.

Paul had to deal with conflicts over several issues that Jesus is shown addressing in the gospels. Consider these questions:

- If Paul knew Jesus had told his followers to pay taxes to Rome (Mark 12:14-17), why not invoke his teaching when addressing the same issue in Romans 13:6-7?

- When making a case for Christian celibacy (1 Cor. 7:1, 7-8, 32-35), why did he not quote Jesus endorsing it in Matthew 19:10-12? [9]

- In discussing the thorny matter of speaking in tongues, why no reference to what Jesus says in Mark 16:17?

- Wouldn't Matthew 18:15-20 have come in handy when Paul was telling his congregants how to handle disciplinary procedure (1 Cor. 5:3-5)?

- Discussing the wretched matter of divorce (1 Cor. 7:15-16), why not bring Jesus (Mark 10:2-9) in on the question? I would have, and so would you.

- Should Christian missionaries expect material support from their converts? Paul offers various arguments, including an analogy to a command to feed your oxen (Deut. 25:4) quoted in 1 Corinthians 9:3-11). Wouldn't it have been simpler and more effective just to quote Jesus (Matt. 10:9-10; Luke 10:9)? [10]

Most think the Pauline letters predate the gospels by decades. Thus the question here is not really why Paul didn't quote our finished gospels. On the standard dating, they hadn't been written yet. But supposedly the teachings of Jesus were circulating by word of mouth and eventually wound up in the gospels.

If such teachings were available to Paul, why on earth would he not have quoted them? Surely he would have! This has led many to infer that there simply were no such teachings making the rounds, that subsequently people began attributing sayings they liked to their Lord and Savior. It would also explain why the gospels ascribe conflicting opinions to Jesus on various topics such as divorce, fasting, and preaching to Gentiles.

One place where Paul might be seen as knowing a command of Jesus is "concerning the unmarried," where he says, "I have no command of the Lord, but I give my opinion as one who by the Lord's mercy is trustworthy" (1 Cor. 7:25). In another, he has a command of the Lord regarding divorce: "To the married I give charge, not I but the Lord, that the wife should not separate from her husband . . . and that the husband should not divorce his wife" (1 Cor. 7:10-11).

Note, however, that he does not say this commandment is from *Jesus*. It could just as well have come directly to him from the Holy Spirit. In light of 1 Corinthians 14:37 ("If anyone thinks that he is a prophet, or spiritual, he should acknowledge that what I am writing to you is a command of the Lord"), this latter pretty much *has* to be what he means. He even says that his knowledge of what happened at the Last Supper was imparted to him directly from "the Lord" (1 Cor. 11:23-25), not from some historical memory.[11]

Paul even says that the Savior received the exalted name "Jesus" (Hebrew *Jehoshua*, "Jehovah is salvation") *after* his enthronement at the right hand of the Father. Here is the *kenosis* hymn in

Philippians 2:5-11, formatted lyrically:

Have this mind among yourselves,
    which is yours in Christ Jesus,
    who, though he was in the form of God,
    did not count equality with God a thing to be grasped,
    but emptied himself,
    taking the form of a servant,
    being born in the likeness of men.

And being found in human form he humbled himself
    and became obedient unto death,
        even death on a cross.

Therefore God has highly exalted him
    and bestowed on him the name
        which is above every name,
    that at the name of Jesus every knee should bow,
        in heaven and on earth and under the earth,
    and every tongue confess that Jesus Christ is Lord,
        to the glory of God the Father.

Notice that "highly exalting him" is paralleled with "bestowing upon him the highest name." Then "bowing at the name of Jesus" is made parallel to "confessing the lordship of Jesus."

The logic is that the bestowal of the throne name "Jesus" is followed at once by the universal acclamation of him who has received that name as a reward for his struggles in human form. But this wouldn't make sense if Paul thought of an earthly savior who had *already* borne the name "Jesus."

So, did Paul really know of a wandering rabbi called Jesus? [12] I wouldn't bet on it. You shouldn't either.

The Hole in Holy History
Nothing from contemporary historians

The gospel Jesus is a superhero with some spectacular first-century super-powers. It's hard to believe *The Daily Planet* didn't cover him. There is no mention of any such character by contemporaries, whether historians or in personal letters.

I am not arguing here that there was no historical Jesus of some kind. If Jesus had been one of many exorcists and faith healers, if he had been a mere prophet or sage, we would not necessarily expect him to have left written echoes. So the literary silence on Jesus doesn't really militate against such a historical figure. But it is fatal for the gospels' Jesus character having existed as a real historical person.

Nobody took note of a man who performed feats like transforming water into wine, walking on water, multiplying food, and stopping storms at sea? Matthew says a report of Jesus raising a ruler's daughter from the dead "went through all that district" (Matt. 9:26), that "crowds marveled" at his casting out a demon and restoring speech (9:33). Yet no secular sources mention even rumors about such things.

"Well, what about Josephus?" the apologist will protest. Josephus was a Jewish historian who wrote at the end of the first century A.D., recounting the Jewish War with Rome and even mentioning a couple of messiahs in connection with it. But no Jesus. What believers like about Josephus is a famous paragraph in our copies of his *Jewish Antiquities* that mentions Jesus as a miracle-working teacher who fulfilled scriptural prophecies and rose from the dead. Josephus, according to this bit of text, even declared him Messiah!

Don't get your hopes up. The second-century theologian Origen of Alexandria did his reading from a much older copy of Josephus than ours, and it did not contain this paragraph. It is patently obvious that this section, famous as the *Testimonium Flavianum*, was fabricated and inserted into Josephus' book by some Christian. The penciling of this paragraph into Josephus' history actually accentuates the problem rather than alleviating it: A poverty of evidence spurred someone into just fabricating evidence.

The other second-century sources mentioning Jesus are merely third-hand reports of what Christians were preaching at that time about their savior (so Cornelius Tacitus and Pliny Secundus) or else are so ambiguous we cannot even be sure they are talking about Jesus Christ (so Suetonius and the Mishnah).

A Christ of Contradictions

The Jesus Christ of the Bible may be the fruit rather than the root of Christianity. He may have originated as a figment of the religious imagination. When we look closely enough, the fingerprints of the human creators and the jagged seams of their work become shockingly evident. They have eluded scrutiny for centuries thanks to the theological spin doctors' mighty feats of contortionist obfuscation.

But "nothing is hidden that shall not be revealed," to borrow from Luke 8:17. Pry their protective fingers from over your eyes. Think about it: What are you defending?

We have seen that the precious gospel of gentle Jesus meek and mild fails to mask an unimaginably cruel message of doom and damnation for most of the human race. Unless, that is, they can somehow persuade themselves that divine mercy, justice, and moral perfection are compatible with genocide, rapine, slaughter, and everlasting hellfire. The contradictions in that turn out to be so severe as to render the gospel of Christ an untenable–indeed *unintelligible*–mishmash of mutual negations.

Is it true? It doesn't even come to that. It would have to be consistent some way or the other even to be judged false! Instead, the whole mess works out to just so much pernicious gibberish. Is it worth the efforts of apologists who are much too clever for their own good, and yours?

Notes

1. Charles H. Talbert, ed., *Reimarus: Fragments*. Trans. Ralph S. Fraser. Lives of Jesus Series (Philadelphia: Fortress Press, 1970), pp.

235, 239-40.

2. Reimarus, pp. 218-20.

3. J. Stuart Russell, *The Parousia: A Study of the New Testament Doctrine of Our Lord's Second Coming* (London: T. Fisher Unwin, 1887; rpt. Grand Rapids: Baker Book House, 1983).

4. G.A. Wells, *Did Jesus Exist?* (London: Elek/Pemberton, 1975), p. 19.

5. Earl Doherty, *The Jesus Puzzle: Did Christianity Begin with a Mythical Christ?* (Ottawa: Canadian Humanist Publications, 1999), pp. 69-70.

6. Wells, *Did Jesus Exist?,* pp. 19-20.

7. G.B. Caird, *Principalities and Powers: A Study in Pauline Theology.* The Chancellor's Lectures for 1954 at Queen's University, Kingston Ontario (Oxford at the Clarendon Press, 1956); Paul Louis Couchoud, *The Creation of the Christ: An Outline of the Beginnings of Christianity.* Trans. C. Bradlaugh Bonner (London: Watts, 1939), p. 70.

8. G.A. Wells, *The Jesus of the Early Christians* (London: Pemberton Books, 1971), p. 132.

9. Wells, *Did Jesus Exist?,* p. 19.

10. *Id.*

11. Hyam Maccoby, *Paul and Hellenism* (London: SCM Press, Philadelphia: Trinity Press International, 1991), pp. 91-92.

12. Couchoud at p. 438.

VII

The Bible Versus the Bible

> The Bible is not the verbally inspired, inerrant word of God; it was just a collection of contradictory, discrepant books that had been written by superstitious ethnocentrics who thought that the hand of God was directing the destiny of the Hebrew people.
>
> —Farrell Till [1]

The world is full of well-meaning people who grant divine authority to an ancient book that, while often wise, does not deserve the idolatrous regard they heap upon it. If the Bible were the book its devotees loudly claim it to be, it would not look as it does to the rest of us who read it with a clear eye.

Fundamentalists try to close the gap by reinterpreting the embarrassing parts. But anyone who claims to believe that it is the "plain sense" or "apparent sense" of the biblical text that is authoritative has no business falling back to less-than-apparent, stretched, contrived, less likely interpretations just to avoid admitting that the Bible contradicts itself. If you can do that, then Martin Luther was wrong in his objection to the medieval Roman Catholics: Why not read anything you *want* into the text—including popes and indulgences?

Ask yourself, as you consider retreating to some far-fetched harmonization, "Don't I know better than this? Would this interpretation look good to me if I weren't looking for some way out of a tight spot?" What good is the Bible if you are willing to sacrifice intellectual integrity to defend it?

I have suggested that Jesus Christ is essentially a piece of the Bible, a character in its larger story, and that is true most of all for fundamentalists for whom Jesus' mission is in large measure to authenticate scripture as a reliable revelation. And this they believe because the trustworthy scripture reliably reports that Jesus said so, something we could not know or verify otherwise. Thus the problems we have highlighted with the biblical Jesus are writ even larger in the wider biblical canon: It, too, is infected with stubborn contradictions that render any claim about "biblical authority" not only false but meaningless. We are obliged to consider some of these mixed signals.

The Pentateuch

The Order of Creation

Genesis 1 has God create plants (vv. 11-12), then various animal species (vv. 20-25). Finally, he creates men and women (vv. 26-27), apparently several, as with the animals, all at the same time. But Genesis 2 has a different order of creation: first a male human (v. 7), then plants (the Garden of Eden, vv. 8-9), then the animals (vv. 18-20) in case any might prove to be suitable company for him, and finally a proper companion, a female human (21-23).

Please note: In the Eden story, God does not merely *show* Adam the animals, as if he had already created them. No, he *creates them on the spot*, from the dust of the ground, even as Adam himself was created. Nor does it say "God *had* made all the creatures from the dust of the ground," as if at some earlier time. It is quite clear that his creating them immediately preceded his showing them to the man.

The Missing Mrs. Cain

Who was Mrs. Cain (Gen. 4:17a)? Cain's sister? Did God suspend the incest taboo as well as any bad genetic effects? Come on. Let's not even bother with such nonsense.

In Genesis 4:1, sure, Cain is the first son of Adam and Eve. But in the rest of the Cain stories it is quite clear that he is *not* supposed to be the first human infant born into an otherwise empty world. For whom did he build the city (v. 17b)? Who is he afraid is going to kill him (4:14)?

These stories all presuppose that Cain lives at a later time when the earth is populated. The editor of Genesis has simply patched together disparate legends about Cain, whether or not they presuppose a consistent time line.

Did you ever watch *Xena: Warrior Princess*? Ever notice how the writers place Xena all over ancient history? In one episode, she meets Galen the physician, who lived in the second century A.D., while in another she is helping to defend Troy in remote antiquity! In another, she pals around with Goliath, about 1000 BC! It's the same way with Cain.

Competing Culture Heroes

Genesis 4:2 depicts Abel as the first shepherd and Cain as the first farmer. But verse 20 makes Jabal the first nomadic herdsman, while in Genesis 9:20, Noah is the first tiller of the soil.

You can't just say it means Noah was the first tiller of the soil after the Flood, because it implicitly exonerates his drunkenness as naïve ignorance. Since no one had ever grown grapes before, he didn't know what would happen if he made wine out of them!

Besides this, Jabal is spoken of as "the father of all who dwell in tents and have livestock" *in the reader's day*, implying unbroken continuity with no Flood interrupting between Jabal and the readers. Isn't it obvious that the Jabal and Jubal stories knew nothing of a worldwide Flood that necessitated a reboot of history? Again, the biblical compiler simply did his best to patch together every scrap of ancient lore and legend he was able to get his hands on.

The Duration of the Flood

Did the Flood last 150 days in all (Gen. 7:24)? Or only 61 (40 days of rain plus three weeks of drainage) as in 8:6-12? Did Noah bring aboard a *single* pair of *all* animal species (6:19-20) or *seven pairs* of kosher animals with *one* pair of non-kosher ones (7:2-3)?

No one is saying this is a stupid mistake made by a single narrator. Actually, the differences are important clues that two older Flood stories have been combined here, one from the Yahwist ("J") Source, the other from the Priestly Code ("P").

The **J** version was Genesis 6:5-8; 7:1-5, 7-10, 12, 16b-17, 22-23; 8:2b-3a, 6-12, 13b, 20-22; 9:18-19. In it, the Flood is caused by rain, and the waters increase for 40 days, taking another three weeks to dry up, a total of 61 days. Noah observes kosher laws, taking aboard a single pair of unclean animal species, seven pairs of kosher species.

The **P** version includes Genesis 6:9-22; 7:6, 11, 13-16a, 18-21, 24; 8:1-2a, 3-5, 13a, 14-19; 9:1-17, 28-29. This time, the waters deepen for 150 days and recede gradually, the whole flood lasting one year, 11 days. The Priestly author knew that kosher laws began much later, so he has Noah, a vegetarian, bring only a single pair of animals (he won't be eating any of them during the voyage). And the Flood results from the gushing up of the subterranean sources of the world ocean.

Who Sold Joseph?

Remember Joseph with the coat of many colors and a lousy bunch of brothers who threw him into a pit? Genesis 37:28 says Joseph was pulled out by Midianites who sold him to Ishmaelites, who in turn sold him into Egyptian slavery. But 37:36 says the Midianites themselves sold him as a slave once *they* got into Egypt.

It won't work to say that the second verse is just summarizing the events of the first, eliminating the middle man for brevity's sake, because verse 36 specifically says the Midianites were in Egypt when *they* sold Joseph into slavery. Our editor had two versions of the Joseph story, one of them fragmentary, and decided to include everything.

The Divine Name

When did people start calling God *Yahweh* (Jehovah, YHWH)? Was it in Enosh's day (Gen. 4:26), before the Flood? Or was it only once Yahweh appeared to Moses at the burning bush (Exod. 6:2-3)?

Some desperate harmonizers will come back with pious nonsense such as "Well, er, you see, they hadn't known the *theological fullness* of the divine name until God revealed himself to

Moses! Yeah, *that's* the ticket!" I'm not even sure I know what that's supposed to mean, but in any case, such hair-splitting subtleties have to be shoe-horned into the text–and you know it! To paraphrase James Taylor: "You just can't [lie] for Jesus."

Resilient Bovines

How many times did the Egyptian cattle die from the Exodus plagues? Looks like three times (Exod. 9:6, 18-26; 12:29)! As the subtitle reads from the classic horror flick *Night of the Living Dead*, "They won't stay dead!"

Well, you might suggest, maybe there were exceptions each time, and it was the survivors that died the next time around. Sorry, but that doesn't work. There were indeed exceptions each time: the cattle owned by the Israelites! God spared theirs–and only theirs! If he had also spared any Egyptian cows, that would have introduced an ambiguity. And that would have totally undermined the lesson being taught to Pharaoh.

Once again, it is not that a single biblical writer made stupid mistakes. No, just the opposite: There were already three different versions of the Plagues story, and our later editor didn't feel at liberty to leave any of it out. The result is blatant contradiction.

Davidic Difficulties

Introducing David

When did King Saul first meet David? When he recruited him as a musician to ease his possession spells (1 Sam. 16:14-23)? Or after the battle with Goliath? (1 Sam. 17:55-58)?

Again, this is not some "mistake." Two sources have been spliced together.

Goliath Shooting Gallery?

Who killed Goliath of Gath? David (1 Sam. 17:48-51) or Elhanan (2 Sam. 21:19)? Or do you think maybe there were two giants from Gath in Philistia who had the same huge armor and gigantic stature? And both were named Goliath?!?

Isn't it obvious that someone thought, "Why waste an exploit like that on the lesser known character Elhanan? Why not add the accolade to David's resume?" But you didn't dare clip the other version (it was sacred tradition, too), so both went in!

Gospel Grief

Dueling Genealogies

Which of the genealogies (Matt. 1:1-17; Luke 3:23-38) of Jesus is correct? Here are Jesus' most immediate paternal ancestors, as claimed by Matthew and then Luke:

1. "*Joseph* the husband of Mary, of whom Jesus was born" agreeing with "the son (as was supposed) of *Joseph.*"

2. "*Jacob* the father of Joseph" vs. "Joseph [was] the son of *Heli.*"

3. "*Matthan* the father of Jacob" vs. "Heli [was] the son of *Matthat.*"

4. "*Eleazar* the father of Matthan" vs. "Matthat [was] the son of *Levi.*"

There is almost no similarity between the two until they finally get back to David, son of Jesse.

Despite what some desperate apologists would like us to believe, neither genealogy is Mary's. Both explicitly trace Jesus' descent through Joseph. And Mark 12:35-37 contradicts both, since in it Jesus denies that the Messiah will be a descendant of David:

And as Jesus taught in the temple, he said, "How can the

scribes say that the Christ is the son of David? David himself, inspired by the Holy Spirit, declared, 'The Lord said to my Lord, Sit at my right hand, till I put thy enemies under thy feet.' David himself calls him Lord; so how is he his son?"

It amazes me that people can try to evade the force of the argument in Mark 12:35-37, as if Jesus were implying that, though he is also David's son, the Messiah must be something greater, too, namely God's son. Listen, that's just rewriting the passage into what you *wish* it had said! The logic is clear: David would never call his own son his Lord, even if that son were the Messiah, just as he would never have called Solomon his Lord, nor would Solomon have called his son Rehoboam "my Lord." That would have violated court rhetoric.

Now, genealogies are notoriously among the most boring portions of scripture. No one can stand to read them through attentively. Admit it: It's kind of like trying to read a couple of pages of the phone book. And that may be why most of us never notice the violent clash between the family tree of Jesus as set forth in Matthew and Luke. It is only once we take a closer look at the difficulties that these columns of near-unpronounceable names start to become interesting.

In the biblical world, genealogies could be extremely important, especially if someone needed a certain pedigree, lineal descent from Good King David, if he were to qualify for the coveted position of Messiah. This is what made it much more than trivial to be able to trace your ancestors. Personally, I don't really care whom I'm descended from because it makes no practical difference. But then I don't think I'm the Messiah! To Christians, however, it matters quite a lot whether Jesus was the Messiah. And so the contradictions between the gospel genealogies constitute a much bigger issue than it might otherwise appear.

Jesus' Parents Lived Where?

Where did Mary and Joseph live before Jesus was born? Bethlehem (as in Matthew) or Nazareth (as Luke has it)? Take a close look at both nativity stories.

In Luke, they dwell in Nazareth, and it is only a special circumstance that takes the couple to Bethlehem where, in the providence of God, Jesus is born.

In Matthew, they live in Bethlehem, where Jesus is born in their home, and the Wise Men visit them at home a couple of years later. Then they flee to Egypt. Upon their subsequent return home, they flee again, this time to Nazareth, where Archelaus will never find them. This, by the way, is preposterous: There's no reason King Herod wouldn't believe his attempt to kill the infant Jesus in Bethlehem was successful, so why would his successor still be gunning for him?

The Voice from the Sky

What did the heavenly voice say to Jesus at his baptism: "*This is* my beloved Son" (Matt. 3:17), addressing the crowd? Or "*You are* my beloved Son" (Mark 1:11; Luke 3:22), speaking privately to Jesus? Did it somehow say both at once, and different people heard it differently?

Careful now! Allowing such a significant variation in the story gets you mighty close to saying there *was* no heavenly voice, that people were hallucinating.

Which Temptation When?

Matthew and Luke have the devil offer Jesus the same three temptations: Turn stones to bread, leap from atop the temple, and sell his soul to gain the kingdoms of the world. So far, so good.

But which did Satan do last: Take Jesus to the temple pinnacle (Luke 4:9) or to a high mountain where he might see the panorama of the world's kingdoms (Matt. 4:8)? The order of episodes in the two gospels is not the same. Faith commitments keep people from admitting what seems plain here: Either Mathew or Luke changed the order of their shared original (the **Q** source) to make what each considered a more climactic ending.

What else could you say? That Satan offered this particular temptation *twice* and that Matthew and Luke each chose one instance of the temptation and ignored the other? Get outta here! Say this sort of stuff, and you're just asking not to be taken seriously! You're letting everybody know that you'll say any nutty thing in order to stick to the party line. You think people can't see that?

Signs to be Observed?

Did Jesus list the signs that would signal the kingdom of God was near (Mark 13:28-30)? Or did he say there would be no advance warning (Luke 17:20-21)?

Maybe we'll just have to wait till we get to heaven–announced by trumpets or otherwise–for the explanation of that one, or any of the others. Fundamentalists often speak as if they look forward to a great seminar to be offered in heaven, in which, let's say, the Patriarch Enoch, master of heavenly secrets, holds forth, untangling all those long-standing stumpers. "Where did Cain get his wife? Would you like to know? May I have the envelope please!"

Too bad that these Bible contradictions and ambiguities will get cleared up only once it is all moot, when you don't really even need a Bible anymore! It's down *here*, in this grimy, sinful, confusing world, where we ostensibly need the guidance of the Bible. If one passage cancels the other out, it is no more useful than firewood that is soaking wet.

Call these "apparent" contradictions if it makes you feel any better. Either way, the text is doing you no good in the here and now. You'll just have to think for yourself–not a bad idea!

Think Fast!

Did Jesus say his disciples would no longer fast (Mark 2:21-22), that they would suspend fasting temporarily (Mark 2:18-20), or that they ought to fast, just not like the hypocrites (Matt. 6:16-18)? Look at the metaphors in Mark: They point in very different directions.

Here is the pertinent part of Mark 2, with emphasis added:

> Now John's disciples and the Pharisees were fasting; and people came and said to him, "Why do John's disciples and the disciples of the Pharisees fast, but your disciples do not fast?" (v. 18)

> And Jesus said to them, "Can the wedding guests fast while the bridegroom is with them? As long as they have the bridegroom with them, they cannot fast. The days will come, when the bridegroom is taken away from them, and then *they will fast in that day*. (vv. 19-20)

> "No one sews a piece of unshrunk cloth on an old garment; if he does, the patch tears away from it, the new from the old, and a worse tear is made. And *no one puts new wine into old wineskins*; if he does, the wine will burst the skins, and the wine is lost, and so are the skins; but new wine is for fresh skins." (vv. 21-22)

The business in verses 21-22 about not putting new wine into ill-fitting old wineskins implies that fasting is outmoded in light of the arrival of God's kingdom. But the analogy of the bridegroom's departure in verses 19-20 implies that it will soon be appropriate to resume fasting.

Mark has combined two mutually exclusive sayings on the same topic, each representing a rival early Christian position on the issue, fraudulently fathered on Jesus. If Jesus was actually on record saying either one, where would the other have come from? Who would have thought he knew better than the Son of God?

Meanwhile, in Matthew 6:16-18, Jesus gives instructions about fasting:

> And when you fast, do not look dismal, like the hypocrites, for they disfigure their faces that their fasting may be seen

by men. Truly, I say to you, they have received their reward. But when you fast, anoint your head and wash your face, that your fasting may not be seen by men but by your Father who is in secret; and your Father who sees in secret will reward you.

It seems a bit odd for him to be telling his disciples how to do something he elsewhere said they don't *have* to do, at least not yet.

Divorce, Jesus Style

Did Jesus allow no excuse for divorce (Mark 10:2-9; Luke 16:18) or just *one* excuse (Matt. 5:31-32; 19:3-9)? Clearly, Matthew saw the difficulties that an absolute ban on divorce was causing, so he emended the gospel text so as to restore the escape-clause of Deuteronomy 24:1.

Does this mean Matthew was "lying" about what Jesus said? Of course not! It just means he regarded the text not as a historical report, but as a new law for Christians, and that law needed to be amended, just as Moses amended the Law so daughters could inherit (Num. 27:1-11). Again, it's a genuine contradiction, and it is easy to see how it came about.

Who Walked on Water?

Was it only Jesus who walked on water, as in Mark 6:45-52 and John 6:15-21? Or did Peter, too, walk on the waves, as in Matthew 14:22-33? Did the other gospel writers just forget about Peter? Were they just running out of ink?

No, of course not. It is a sermonic, edifying addition, to urge readers to keep their faith fixed on Jesus during troubled times. That's a point the added material makes quite well, but it's not a part of the story according to Mark and John.

Demonic Duet?

Did Jesus heal *one* Gerasene demoniac (Mark 5:1-20; Luke 8:26-39), or *two* (Matt. 8:28-34)? Now, don't try telling me it was two but that Mark and Luke picked their favorite demoniac to mention without actually denying the presence of another! What sense would that make? Rather think of Matthew's editorial tendency to double single items in his sources, such as the pair of blind men modeled on Mark's Bartimaeus story, and the doubling of the donkeys Jesus rides into Jerusalem (see below).

Double Dumb Ass on You

The redeemer rides in, rodeo-style

Did Jesus ride one beast into Jerusalem (Mark 11:1-10; Luke 19:28-38; John 12:12-15)? Or two, somehow, at the same time (Matt. 21:1-9)? Isn't it more natural to understand Matthew as following the pattern of rabbinical over-interpretation of biblical parallelism?

When a poetic couplet in scripture said one thing in two ways ("mounted on a donkey, the foal of an ass"), the rabbis ignored poetic convention and took it in an exaggerated literal sense so as to pump more "detailed information" out of the Bible. Didn't make much sense in ordinary language? They didn't care. Neither did Matthew when he interpreted Zechariah 9:9:

Rejoice greatly, O daughter of Zion!
Shout aloud, O daughter of Jerusalem!
Lo, your king comes to you;
triumphant and victorious is he,
humble and riding on an ass,
on a colt the foal of an ass.

The Temple Ruckus

When did Jesus cleanse the temple? At the start of his ministry, as in John 2:13-17? Or was it at the end, as in all three other gospels (Mark 11:15-19; Luke 19:45-48; Matt. 21:12-13)? Since it sealed his doom, he couldn't have done it twice.

Denying a Blue Streak

Whom, and in what order, did Peter answer when he denied Jesus three times (Mark 14:66, 69, 70; Matt. 26:69, 71, 73; Luke 22:56, 58, 59; John 18:17, 25, 26)? And don't tell me he denied him six or eight times, just to get them all in! The text says three!

Jesus doesn't predict to Peter, "Before the rooster crows tomorrow, you will have denied me *at least* three times!" And if it was prophecy "set in stone," why didn't Jesus predict the exact number, if three wasn't it?

Post-Passion Problems

Double Jeopardy with Judas

Did anyone know what became of Judas Iscariot? Matthew says Judas had second thoughts and, mortified at what he had done, hanged himself. He had returned the thirty silver sheckels to the priests who, however, could not put the money back into the Temple treasury, since it was tainted, being bounty money. So they used it for a charitable act, buying a field to open as a cemetery for indigents (seeing to the burial of the friendless dead was a major act of charity in ancient Judaism). Because of this, the place became known as The Field of Blood, on account of the "blood money" which purchased it (Matt. 27:3-10).

So far so good, but Acts 1:15-20 has Peter tell quite a different story. Now it appears that *Judas himself* used the bounty money to buy a field, and, taking possession of it, he swelled up and exploded, guts flying everywhere, like Mr. Creosote in Monty Python's *The Meaning of Life*. The Greek word used here can mean either "falling headlong" or "swelling up." Papias, second-century bishop of Hierapolis, implied the latter, saying that Judas ballooned up to grotesque proportions, his lumbering form filled with pus and infested with maggots.

Apologists would have us believe there is a single coherent narrative of Judas' death, and that Matthew and Acts each tell just half of it. Supposedly, then, Judas still did hang himself but used cheap kite string that instantly snapped, causing his body to drop to the ground below, whereupon he was disemboweled upon impact. That's quite a stretch, no pun intended. In order for his plummeting form to generate sufficient momentum to splatter, he would've had to hang himself not in a field but from a tree leaning out over a precipice.

Plus, you'd still have to explain how both the Sanhedrin *and* Judas bought the field. Don't try telling me that Judas' providing money used by others to make the purchase qualifies as him (indirectly) buying the plot of ground. Maybe if he'd left instructions in a suicide note that the priests should buy the field, but that's ridiculous. Besides this, Judas and the priests are said to have had different purposes in mind for the real estate.

And there is the matter of the property's name: "Field of Blood." Matthew says it commemorated the use of blood money to buy the field, while Acts says it received the name because of the disgusting bloodbath that ensued there. Face it: This is a blatant contradiction. If you still think it's not, well, you can twist the Bible into saying anything you want it to say, like a "nose of wax" as Luther put it.

Crucified When? Twice?

Was Jesus crucified on Passover (John 19:14, 31) or on the day after? (In the other gospels, the Last Supper is already a Passover meal.) No doubt John changed it to make a theological, symbolic point: Jesus dies as the new Passover lamb.

It isn't some kind of stupid mistake; nobody's charging that. No, it's a purposeful change to a literary text. The reason evangelicals don't like to admit that sort of thing is that they are afraid they won't know where to draw the line between fiction and history in the gospels. They're right! But just because something may make things more complicated for you doesn't mean it's not true.

Some point out that certain sectarian Jews (like the Essenes) held to a different calendar that had them celebrating Passover a full day before their fellow Jews, and that the gospels show Jesus observing this unorthodox calendar. Thus for them it *was* Passover, though for most Jews, Passover would be the next day. So the Last Supper was a Passover seder as far as Jesus and his disciples were concerned, but Jesus was crucified on everybody else's Passover.

Alas, that won't work, for John does not make the Last Supper a Passover celebration of any kind. When he refers to Passover, it is that which the Sanhedrin and all Jews are about to celebrate. John even says the disciples, sitting at table at the Last Supper, knew Passover was not that very night, but the next. They thought Judas left the table to go buy something needed for Passover, which therefore could not have been the very meal they were eating right then (John 13:29).

Did the Women See the Risen Jesus?

Did the women at the tomb behold Jesus himself (as happens in Matthew 28:9) or only the two men (Luke 24:1-8)? Did most women see nothing (John 20:2), leaving Mary to see Jesus by herself (John 20:11-17)? Is this a minor difference of trivial detail, as apologists would tell us? That is absurd: imagine the reaction if two witnesses in a murder trial couldn't agree on whether the suspect was there with them on the night of the crime!

Jesus First Appeared to Whom?

The sudden appearance of Jesus amidst the flabbergasted disciples in Luke 24:36-43 and John 20:19-23 appears to be the initial resurrection appearance. But so does the appearance on the Sea of Tiberias in John 21:1-13, with v. 14 being an editorial harmonization. Which one was?

Jesus First Appeared Where?

Did the risen Jesus appear only in the environs of Jerusalem (Luke 24:13, 49) or only in Galilee (Mark 16:7 and Matt. 28:7, 10, 16)? Did the angel tell the women, "Remember how he said he would meet you in Galilee?" (Mark 16:7)? Or "Remember how, *when he was in* Galilee, he told you the son of man must rise," etc. (Luke 24:6)?

Did the Women Make Their Report?

Did the women flee the tomb and tell no one what they had seen (Mark 16:8) or did they tell the disciples after all (Matt. 28:8; Luke 24:10; John 20:18)? The Longer Ending of Mark is of course absent in the earliest manuscripts. Mark had no resurrection appearances. How *could* he, when he plainly says the women failed to tell Peter and the others to meet him?

This contradiction is extremely important. It means that Matthew, Luke, and John didn't like Mark's ending and changed it. Everything they have happen after the empty tomb story is predicated on changing Mark's ending. This has to mean whatever they added is fiction.

And it's no trivial addition. This is the *resurrection* we are talking about. "If Christ has not been raised, your faith is futile and you are still in your sins" (1 Cor. 15:17).

Two Ascensions?

Did Jesus ascend to heaven Easter evening (Luke 24:13-52) or forty days later (Acts 1:3, 9)? Did he keep bouncing between earth and heaven?

See the Light or Hear the Voice?

Did Paul's companions hear the voice of Jesus without seeing anyone or anything (Acts 9:7)? Or did they see the light but not hear the voice (Acts 22:9)?

Perhaps there is a goof in Acts. But it may simply be a case of Luke varying the details so the story remains fresh for the reader, who is, after all, hearing it for the third time! (It's also in Acts 26.) If that's what Luke did, he certainly wasn't very concerned about getting the facts straight, so we have to wonder what other liberties he took.

A Christ Divided Cannot Stand

There remain many, many more Bible contradictions, so many that, if they were all to be written down, the whole world would be filled with the books that must be written. But these have been written so that you may realize that biblical inerrantism is a false and misleading approach to the Bible, and that, realizing that, you may renounce it and take a more realistic approach. You know, thinking for yourself.

Let's return to the question of divorce for a moment. As a pious Christian you naturally want the guidance of Jesus on the matter. "Can I get a divorce without disobeying Jesus?" But you're stuck, aren't you? Two gospels have Jesus answering "No," while a third says, "All right, in one kind of situation, yes."

If you obey one version, you seem to be disobeying the other. How does the infallible wisdom of Jesus put you ahead of the game? What advantage does it give you above the poor dumb heathen? It may be the inspired word of God, but what is it worth if it leaves you caught in the dilemma: to divorce, or not to divorce? Basically, you've just got an unsolvable riddle with a halo over its head. Why not just turn a few pages and heed Jesus' words in Luke 12:57: "Why do you not judge for yourselves what is right?"

Notes

1. Farrell Till, "From Preacher to Skeptic," in *Leaving the Fold: Testimonies of Former Fundamentalists*, ed. Edward Babinski (Amherst, NY: Prometheus Books, 2003).

VIII

No Need for That Hypothesis

> We are explaining more every day. We are understanding more
> every day; consequently your God is growing smaller every day.
>
> —Robert G. Ingersoll, *Lecture on Gods*

Did you know that the word "epilepsy" is based on the Greek words for "seized upon"? Uh . . . by whom or what? *Demons*, that's who. The ancients looked at people in the midst of epileptic fits and made the best guess available to them. The poor epileptic looked as if he were no longer in control of his body, and indeed he was not. So who had grabbed the steering wheel? Somebody invisible yet obviously malevolent; in short, a demon.

It wasn't a stupid guess. But it turned out to be mistaken once we learned something about electrical discharges in the brain. Look, not even Plato and Aristotle could have known anything about that. But now that we do, we can take a second look at the gospel accounts of Jesus exorcising epileptics, then move through a brief overview of science and the Bible to arrive at the issue of *free will*. That, as we shall see, presents another dilemma for Christianity and its idea of eternal judgment by a just God.

Supernatural and Superfluous

We know now that yelling at spooks is not going to cure epilepsy and never did. But modern medicine can at least treat the symptoms because, knowing the actual cause, we can begin doing something to solve the problem. So what happens to the ancient belief in evil spirits? It proves to be superfluous. The cause is more mundane. We don't need "demons" as an etiology for the affliction.

Can you imagine a group of doctors on *Mystery Diagnosis* throwing in the towel and saying, "I don't know—I guess call in an exorcist!" No, they don't do that because they know that appealing to the supernatural is just tantamount to exclaiming, "God only knows how to cure *this*!" It is simply an admission of ignorance.

In a famous encounter that took place around 1802, the emperor Napoleon Bonaparte asked his royal astronomer Pierre Simon Laplace if he'd factored God into his theories of the universe and its origin. Laplace's reply proved to be more significant than any of his particular theories: "I have no need for that hypothesis." [1]

It wasn't exactly that science proved God had nothing to do with the design of the world. Rather, it showed that any such role for God is superfluous. It is a fifth wheel. There is no blank for him to fill. It's as if God were to say, "Here, Laplace. Let me help you explain that," only to be told, "Uh, that's okay, old fellow. I think I've got it all worked out."

This has been the recurring pattern when it comes to God and science. As scientists of all kinds gain more and more knowledge of how things work, there is less and less temptation to use God as a stop-gap, a place holder until a real answer comes along. And it turns out that is all God ever was.

It's exactly like the famous cartoon by Sidney Harris, where one lab-coated scientist is proudly showing a colleague a backboard full of chalked formulae. Almost hidden amid the numbers and symbols is an empty space with a note that says, "Then a miracle occurs." His colleague remarks, "I think you should be more explicit here in step two." That's no joke! Calling on miracles is what we used to do until we got a little clearer on scientific method. But this approach resulted in one embarrassment after another.

Automation kept putting the Almighty out of one job after another, giving him a pretty big collection of pink slips. It has now become more than clear that every time we say, "There's just no naturalistic explanation for so-and-so, so it must have been a miracle!" what we are doing is to bank on ignorance. Had science been content to "explain" illness as due to evil spirits, we never would have sought a better answer (namely germs, bacteria, viruses, etc.) and, with it, a cure.

Science has gotten its act together. It's *religion* that insists on sticking with medievalism. For instance, "Intelligent Design" Creationists tell us that evolution could not account for the appearance of complex organs or organisms. Evolution, so science says, proceeds by a very slow, gradual accumulation of tiny modifications. If one new little quirk enables a critter to get more food and to live longer, it can have more offspring, each carrying the new trait. They will have the same advantage, each living longer to produce more offspring "in his own image." Thus it will contribute a larger share to its species' next generation.

In time, its heirs will dominate the species. As more modifications pop up, the cycle repeats itself until the species is very far from where it started, and we are dealing with a brand new species. It works just fine on its own. You don't need God intervening, tweaking the DNA to produce "new and improved" models.

But Intelligent Design propagandists, motivated by Christian fundamentalism, don't much like this kind of talk. So they say that gradual accumulation of tiny changes couldn't do the trick. You couldn't get something like a functioning eye by incremental addition of micro-changes. Half an eye wouldn't have any survival advantage over a quarter-eye. A creature that popped up with a half-eye wouldn't have any better chance of surviving long enough to stack the genetic deck for the next generation. You'd have to have a whole eye, right? So the complete, fully functional eye must have appeared all at once. And in that case, it must have been the invention, like the camera was, of an intelligent designer. And you bet they have an applicant in mind for the job! A guy named Dr. Jehovah.

The trouble for ID fans is that *any* degree of greater light-sensitivity would prove advantageous for survival. We know this because we still *have* species with every possible "shade" of light-sensitivity, from microbes to eagles.[2] Sorry, you just don't need God. And if you insist on cramming God into the picture, you're just mucking up science.

And pity poor Jehovah! For him, it's still the Great Depression: He listlessly shuffles from one store, one factory, to another, looking for employment–but there are just no openings! Let's take a closer look at the jobs report, shall we?

Getting the Gospel off the Ground
Cultural evolution and Christianity

The rise of the Christian religion was certainly a dramatic success story. How are we to explain it? Christians often boast that the historic success of their faith is a proof of its divine origin. How else could it have grown from a tiny band of persecuted martyrs to the official religion of the Roman Empire in a mere three centuries? (Never mind that pretty much the same question can be raised in the cases of Buddhism, Zoroastrianism, and Islam.)

But this is really pretty ironic, especially when you go on to claim, as some apologists do, that Christianity was so repugnant, so stupid-sounding, with nothing to commend it, that it would take nothing less than divine intervention to explain how it could have attracted anyone. One can only reply that, with "defenders" like these, who needs critics?

Sociologist Rodney Stark[3] gives aid and comfort to self-congratulatory Christians in one respect but not in another. He debunks the notion of a miraculous expansion of Christianity by means of the Holy Spirit. The attested growth rates of analogous modern faiths (40% growth per decade, like the Moonies and the Mormons), he says would easily explain the population percentages of Christians attested century by century for the Roman Empire. Christian population growth was healthy but nothing out of the ordinary. We need no suspension of natural law to explain the success of the movement.

It is much simpler to point to the attractive features of the faith to explain its expansion. And if you're trying to make your case for the Christian religion, this is certainly the one to make. Miracles, after all, aren't the only game in town.

Stark argues that it was the distinctiveness of Christian belief that fostered the religion's success. Christians acted quite differently from other religions, and history rewarded them for it.

First, Christians loathed abortion and infanticide, both quite common in their environment. The result was that they had a significantly larger proportion of women in their ranks. Why?

People only exposed baby girls, literally putting them to the curb with the trash, because parents feared they'd never marry all of them off. They'd be stuck with all those pretty mouths to feed forever. Christians took the risk, so they had more daughters to marry off.

This development gave women greater freedom and opportunities for leadership roles, something that happens naturally in a social group with more women. By contrast, where women are scarce, as they often were in the Hellenistic world thanks to the disastrously bone-headed eugenics policies of the Roman state, they are more likely to be sequestered and rigidly controlled. Similarly, with a greater share of women to marry off, the Christian community stood to increase its numbers by a simple process of "interfaith" marriages with the non-Christian spouses converting.

Second, Christians believed they were duty-bound to love their neighbors as themselves, whether part of the household of faith or not. Accordingly, Christians cared for the sick and the helpless in times of famine, plague, and crisis, of which there were many. Nor is this mere Christian propaganda. The emperor Julian the Apostate (who tried his best to revive a declining paganism) made a concerted and well-documented effort to copy the Christian social ethic in his revivified heathenism, but to no avail. We hear of pagan clergy running for the hills in times of emergency: "Every man for himself!" Christians had a greater proportion of their own sick nursed back to health. But they also came to the rescue of others when no one else would. You can imagine a lot of these grateful pagans converted to Christ, swelling the ranks of Christianity.

Third, there was the courage of Christian martyrs. Outsiders admired them, and Tertullian, a Carthaginian theologian of the late second century, described how the martyrs were "seed," producing new crops of converts who reckoned that a faith worth dying for must be worth living for, too.

Fourth, the exclusivism of early Christianity had significant "survival value" for the movement. Their monotheistic "intolerance" made Christian faith an all- or-nothing commitment, not a mere membership in one more salvific moose lodge like Mithraism, the Isis cult, etc. All of those others were mutually tolerant, interpenetrating, redundant, and thus commanding little loyalty. People typically got themselves initiated into as many of these religions as they could afford. They were trying to cover their bets, get in good with as many deities and saviors as they could. This implied a lack of confidence in any of the various salvation insurance policies.

But, unlike the others, Christianity required new members to repudiate all the other cults. This was conducive to a greater confidence in the one bet you'd placed all your chips on. What this means in terms of numbers is that every time a member of these other cults switched over to Christianity, Christianity gained one, while Mithraism, the Isis cult, the Attis cult and any others the new Christian had belonged to now lost one. Several pagan groups lost a member (the same one!) every time Christianity converted one.

None of this implies that Christianity is the one true religion, only that certain beliefs and policies have measurable social results. Again, look at the great success of the Mormons, based on early polygamous mating patterns and later beneficence and welfare structures. Or look at the famous (though much-debated) connection between the Calvinistic work ethic and the rise of Capitalism.[4]

Despite a dubious rap sheet in subsequent centuries, Christians have a lot of things to be proud of when they look back at the rise of their religion. But a miracle isn't one of them.

Determined to be Free
Predestination vs. Free Will

Here I want to argue in a slightly different vein, but I'll be sticking to the main theme of this chapter. Our apparent moral autonomy and freedom of the will, on the basis of which, we are told, God will one day judge us, is thoroughly explainable in terms of purely natural factors, which I will list and discuss. This means there is no "ghost in the machine," no divine spark within us.[5]

Now, it seems to us that our actions, words, and decisions just appear spontaneously, out of nowhere. So much so, in fact, that it sometimes seems to us that we are merely observing what comes out of our mouths, helplessly watching ourselves act, as if it were someone else. But this is a trick of perspective. Our conscious selves are more the fruit than the root.

Consider this reality about your existence: You obviously had no say about being brought into it. No free will there. That might sound like a pat truism, but there is more to it. Your DNA, the recipe for making your body and brain what they are, was not of your choosing.

But that DNA inheritance sure does *dictate* your choosing. Long-term studies of identical twins who were separated at birth to grow up in very different environments reveal shocking correspondences between them decades later. Again and again, it turns out that such men had married similar-looking wives with the same names. They'd wind up driving the same make of car, chewing the same brand of gum, etc., etc. Pretty scary! Looks like our genetic make-up controls an awful lot of our choices. It's not as if we *feel* any lack of free choice, but rather that our genes determine what it is that we truly desire and choose.

But this is not to say that genetic inheritance determines everything. Our environment and experiences, in the womb and for many years after, also shape us. Over time they become more amenable to our control, but in many important respects they remain largely beyond our control.

Did you choose the religion in which you were raised? Did you control meeting your friends, your mate? Your occupational opportunities? Think of a thousand other things that were quite beyond your control but which were hugely influential in making you who you are today.

Of course, some experiences are much more significant than others. That you had an itch once has no discernible effects. But the *you* who you were in the beginning has become a different *you* over time and at various points in your life. You would not decide today as you would have decided at 18, 25 or 40.

Now, do you agree that the *you* that now exists at this moment is entirely the product, the result, of the foregoing factors? They would seem to be pretty comprehensive. If so, it follows that any changes in these factors would have resulted in a different you today. The *you* that freely decides at any moment is thus not a *you* free from these determining factors, but rather one that is dependent on them for the choices you make. Had they been different, your choices might be different.

We can acknowledge the truth of all this, and yet we *experience* having free will. We "know" our decisions are our own. Is that nothing but a pathetic illusion? No. On one level we *are* free. This is because we are acting in accord with the law of our being, wherever it came from. We are delighted to obey our inclinations, wherever we got them. To do otherwise would be merely to kick against the goads, not really freedom, mere defiance of whomever issues commands we find abhorrent. The factors that have "predestined" us are not compulsions that our already-established selves resent. It is rather that these factors (heredity, environment, previous experiences) have made us the individuals we are, liking what we like, wanting what we want, valuing what we value.

We have been dealt a particular hand of cards, and it is up to us to play them. Even *how* we play them has been determined by a thousand previous factors that have, e.g., predisposed us to take risks or not to. These choices have not been truly ours anyway since they were programmed into us. But we are not conscious of all these factors in the present moment.

We might compare it to special effects in a movie. Personally, I never watch those pesky TV specials on "The Making of *Star Wars*" or "Behind *The Lord of the Rings*" because I don't want to spoil the magic of seeing space battles, light sabers, ents and orcs, dragons and miracles. I don't want to see the strings on the puppets. Likewise, I don't want to see stage magicians explain how they *really* performed their tricks. I want the thrill of mystery and marvel. And it is the same with the experience, the "illusion" if you will, of free choice and free will.

It seems as if my decisions and actions proceed out of the void of undetermined freedom, though they don't. They were dictated in advance several steps back in a shaping process largely invisible to me. The proof of the pudding is in the eating. The cook knows what ingredients went into it and how it was made. The diner may not know that, but he knows it tastes great! And it *does*! It needn't have just have appeared on the plate out of thin air, though it might as well have for all I can tell, being utterly ignorant of the culinary arts.

So I guess I'm saying it doesn't matter to me if we are totally and absolutely free. It works well enough for me to *feel* that I am. But it sure does make a difference for Christian doctrine, which tells us that one day God will judge us on the basis of the choices we made here on earth. Now *that* makes sense only if we really had options.

Every summons to repentance, whether in the Bible or in modern evangelistic crusades, assumes the hearer is capable of deciding to heed it. All Christian exhortation plainly presupposes that one has the freedom to choose the good over the evil. Otherwise, what on earth is the point? Even Calvinists believe this is the case, perhaps surprisingly given their belief in predestination. They do not deny that the sinner makes the choice to repent and believe; they just say that somehow the decision was also God's on our behalf, and that otherwise we could not make the decision.

But isn't it a blatant contradiction to juxtapose predestination and free will in this manner? They appear to be mutually exclusive, but Calvinists say they embrace both simultaneously. They call it an "antinomy." But that's just a cop-out. I call it "doublethink."

If our choices were predetermined by heredity and environmental conditioning, could we really have acted otherwise than we did? Even the exceptional individual who manages to escape ghetto poverty and nihilism has been enabled to do so by some genetic endowment or early influence that gave Condoleeza Rice or Charles Payne the hope and ambition to beat the odds.

I don't know about you, but I am impatient at the clemency shown by juries to murderers, rapists, etc., because of their upbringing and early traumas. "Poor thing!" Maybe so, but we can't just let them off the hook because we can imagine walking a mile in their shoes. We have to take into account the social context in which we live. We cannot allow it to dissolve into chaos by being "soft on crime," by being "bleeding hearts."

We *must* adopt the operating assumption that criminals are responsible for their actions, no matter *what* it was that caused them to become criminals. Their freedom to do right and wrong, and their responsibility for doing wrong, are a necessary legal fiction. We cannot go back and change their tragic pasts. We can deal only with their guilty present and their likely dangerous futures.

But God is under no such necessity. Once I die and stand before God, or once Judgment Day arrives and we all face the music, there will be no more need to reckon with the social repercussions of our acts. God will be at liberty to consider the case of every single sinner, each murderer, rapist, kidnapper, swindler, politician, on each case's own merits and demerits. And in that context, how can God condemn someone who ultimately was a "special effect," a character in a novel written by unknown authors? "Shall not the judge of all the earth do right?" (Gen. 18:25).

Obviously, this is a secular, scientific version of the ancient doctrine of divine predestination, a teaching that has always provoked righteous indignation even among believers:

What shall we say then? Is there injustice on God's part? By no means! For he says to Moses, "I will have mercy on whom I have mercy, and I will have compassion on whom I have compassion." So it depends not upon man's will or exertion, but upon God's mercy. For the scripture says to Pharaoh, "I have raised you up for the very purpose of showing my power in you, so that my name may be proclaimed in all the earth." So then he has mercy upon whomever he wills, and he hardens the heart of whomever he wills.

You will say to me then, "Why does he still find fault? For who can resist his will?" But who are you, a man, to answer back to God? Will what is molded say to its molder, "Why have you made me thus?" Has the potter no right over the clay, to make out of the same lump one vessel for beauty and another for menial use? What if God, desiring to show his wrath and to make known his power, has endured with much patience the vessels of wrath made for destruction, in order to make known the riches of his glory for the vessels of mercy, which he has prepared beforehand for glory. (Rom. 9:14-23)

Good question, bad answer. Bad, that is, if you think it justifies God's behavior. The text admits that we are screwed: God has every right to create people as logs for the eternal fire. The passage admits that free will is mockery and futility, that it is not free choice that results in damnation, but only the decree of God.

If we had genuine metaphysical freedom, the kind possessed by the self-created or uncreated God, that would be the empty gap in the middle of the vast formula on the blackboard. That would be the miracle filling the hole in a worldly chain of cause and effect. But there is, again, no such miracle. We can understand human behavior without that hypothesis. And without it, there can be no justice in God's judgment.

Notes

1. Alas, this ringing statement to Napoleon is apocryphal. The Wikipedia article for Laplace discusses some conflicting accounts of what he actually said.

2. George Gaylord Simpson, *The Meaning of Evolution* (New York: New American Library, 1951), pp. 58-63. Typically, the arguments of Christian apologists have been refuted decades (if not centuries!) before today's apologists put them forth.

3. Rodney Stark, *The Rise of Christianity: A Sociologist Reconsiders History* (Princeton: Princeton University Press, 1996).

4. On the whole, Stark's explanations for the success of Christianity appear to mirror those of E.R. Dodds in *Pagan and Christian in an Age of Anxiety: Some Aspects of Religious Experience from Marcus Aurelius to Constantine* (New York: W.W. Norton, 1970).

5. It is what Jacques Derrida called "the myth of the voice." J. Claude Evans, *Strategies of Deconstruction: Derrida and the Myth of the Voice*, Minnesota Archive Editions (Minneapolis: University of Minnesota Press, 1991).

Conclusion

The Great Noon

> And "selfless"–that is how all these world-weary cowards and cross-marked spiders wanted themselves, for good reasons. But for all these the day is now at hand, the change, the sword of judgment, *the great noon*: much shall be revealed there. And whoever proclaims the ego wholesome and holy, and selfishness blessed, verily, he will also tell what he knows, foretelling: "Verily, it is at hand, it is near, the great noon!"
>
> —Friedrich Nietzsche, *Thus Spoke Zarathustra*[1]

Elisabeth Kübler Ross, in her influential book *Death and Dying*, sets out a typical progression of stages of reaction people go through when they receive the news that they are soon going to die.

- First is *denial.* "No, it can't be! Those must be somebody else's X-rays!"

- Second comes *anger.* "Why me? How could God do this to me!?"

- Third is *bargaining.* "God, if you get me out of this, I promise I'll become a missionary!" "Look, I'll change my diet and stop smoking! That ought to take care of it, right, Doc?"

- Fourth is *acceptance*, "taking it philosophically." You assess your life, what you have accomplished, or failed to. You resolve to settle grudges with alienated relatives, etc.

I think the same thing happens when people begin to lose their faith. They react initially with denial: "It's just Satan trying to deceive me!" An interest in apologetics serves this denial, which may turn into anger at the author or the professor who planted the seeds of doubt. "They're trying to destroy my faith! Those lousy no-good atheists!"

But then, with further thought, doubters begin to see the validity of some arguments against Christianity or the accuracy of the Bible, and they start negotiating with themselves. "Okay, maybe the Bible contains errors on scientific or historical matters, but it's still infallible on matters of doctrine!" And it ends in resignation. "Okay, I give up. What's next?"

Indeed, what *is* next? I believe the crisis of faith that so many individuals are undergoing is also overtaking our culture as a whole. So let's widen the scope a bit. It may turn out that the collapse of our traditional faiths will be a scattering of a thick, gray cloud cover, and that we will find ourselves blinking at a brilliance of sunlight we had forgotten exists.

As I have studied religion–specifically the anthropology, the sociology, and the history of religions–I have developed a sense of trends, of historical-cultural evolution. And I believe that the direction of cultural evolution is towards radical religious pluralism, then on to secularism in which religion will either wither away entirely or will become marginalized to the point of social irrelevance. First let me set forth the signs of the end.

In his great book *Thus Spake Zarathustra*, Friedrich Nietzsche speaks of the coming of the Great Noon, when all things will be laid bare. In a related passage, the Madman passage in *The Gay Science*, he unleashes a similar revelation, the apocalypse of the Death of God. The two are one, for it is only when the shroud of divine cobwebs is thrust aside that the beacon light can be seen.

We are heading for the Great Noon, a cultural culmination of sorts, an elucidation, a universal clarification. Myth will not become fact, don't get me wrong. There will never be a final revelation of the Truth. We will never "know even as we are known." We will never see "face to face." But at least the Dark Age of spiritual slavery will have ended. There will be no Utopia, though we should continue to pursue one.

It is not that religion's passing will free mankind of such a bane that a Golden Age will ensue. No, I think that religion makes so little difference in most people's behavior now that they will have found other reasons to behave well or badly, and things will be just as confused as they are now. Most of today's confusion, after all, hardly stems from religion. Look at Washington!

The Great Noon has not come and will not come in its flood-tide fullness probably for some centuries. But the Great Dawn began, centuries ago. We call it the Enlightenment. It was the time when the autonomy of reason was proclaimed. When all authorities were overthrown and humanity first felt itself to have reached maturity. Immanuel Kant sounded the clarion call: "Dare to know!"

And from that time forward, autonomous science, philosophy, and historical criticism have marched forward to a new age, to the Great Noon. The Enlightenment ushered in that period, that condition, that state of consciousness we call Modernity.

As science advanced relentlessly, winning campaign after campaign, the bankrupt forces of magic, superstition, supernaturalism, dogma, and ecclesiastical authority all received their fatal blow. Their days are numbered, and the strength they now seem to have in a time of resurgent credulity is only the futile panic of the dragon who has lost the war in heaven. Being cast down to earth, he rages mightily, for he knows that his time is short!

The advance of reason, research, scientific method, and the resultant technology have dealt supernatural, mythic religion a blow from which it can never recover. It is all too obvious that gods do not pull switches to start rainstorms and earthquakes. Providence and miracle are the last refuges of wishful thinking. All over the world, wherever technology has gone, it has eroded traditional religious faith, bringing a scientific way of thinking that impacts a society even if it is not shared by all the individuals there or to the same extent by all.

That is why resurgent Islamic fundamentalism is on the war-path, because their own societies are slipping away from them, and they hope in one last desperate gambit to force the lid back on Pandora's Box. All such "revitalization movements" are doomed to failure. It is too late in the first minute they organize themselves!

Pluralism is another aspect of modernity, facilitated by

immigration and communication. In traditional societies, religious belief was the atmosphere everyone breathed. It was the ideological rationale for all the manners, mores, laws, and customs of the society. It was impossible to doubt. Doing so seemed insane.

But that changes forever once you find yourself away from the old cognitive neighborhood. As soon as you realize plenty of other people hold different beliefs with the same self-evident certainty that *you* take for granted, and with as little justification, everything has changed forever. You can never again take it for granted that the old ways are right.

And the better you get to know other individuals who believe in other things, the more your belief in *anything* is going to be relativized. You can't come to know someone who earnestly lives another faith and smugly condemn him to hell. Stereotypes can't survive such close contact. You may start by making exceptions for individuals you know, but eventually you're going to have to put two and two together. You eventually will conclude that all beliefs are true in some vague metaphorical sense, but little else. You will agree that common moral values are all that matter.

You can throw up walls of defense against this conclusion by fortifying a fortress mentality, refusing to think about the troublesome truth. Or you can segregate yourself from the larger society, having as little to do with it as possible and spending as much time among fellow believers as possible—going to church three times a week, having no close friends who are non-believers, etc.

But few are going to be able to make a go of either strategy after a while. It becomes clearer and clearer that we can understand the working of the world without the hypothesis of religion. You don't need God to explain anything anymore. It is in fact difficult to figure out what difference it could be making in the scheme of things if there *is* a God!

If resurgent fundamentalism is a last gasp, the mealy-mouthed mewlings of liberal religion are death rattles, too. The whole enterprise of liberal religion is to humanize religion, to temper it with modern psychology, to use it for political engagement, to make it less subject to fanaticism and less arbitrary in its behavior. Liberal theology rationalizes, naturalizes, ethicizes.

In short it evacuates itself of everything distinctively religious! It, too, is moribund. Everyone knows the staid liberal churches are dying a terrible lingering death. They question their identity, their reason for being, all the while parroting kindergarten platitudes about their "mission." But sociological surveys indicate that all white denominational churches are in big trouble in the next generation.

Even the fundamentalist mega-churches have apparently renounced any distinctly religious content in favor of financial advice, family values, etc.

Modern technology makes supernaturalism increasingly and inevitably incredible. The drawing together of the global village is bringing about a radically pluralistic world culture (sadly, to a great degree, American pop culture). And in such a world, traditional creeds no longer function as charters for unanimous cultural universes of meaning. For us to live together in these plural societies we have to sacrifice religion to privatization. That is, we have to find a non-religious common ground to provide a charter for life together. It can't be based on religion since we don't agree on that. So it becomes based on common moral values. It is based on a Social Compact, a lowest common denominator of staying out of each other's faces.

In such a world, one's religion must be reduced to a private preference, a hobby, a closet belief like the belief in astrology which has no real effect on any other area of life. One's religious allegiance, such as it is, must shrink to something like an ethnic heritage. But even this is not stable, because what happens to ethnic identities in a plural society? There are militant enclaves of various ethnic groups, but these exist solely to stem the inevitable tide of mixture and assimilation. Again, a defensive last gasp.

Interfaith marriage is rapidly breaking down the barriers between different ethnic and different religious identities. Once a Christian marries a Jew, it is simply not an option for either to think that the other is damned, a member of a false religion. Such a belief would function as a barrier to love.

And then of course there is the big question: How do we raise the children? They will correctly perceive that each religion is merely a different set of ethnic, cultural trappings. Or they get raised as secularists, with no religion. Or they get raised as Unitarians, again with no religion. Don't you see what must happen sooner or later?

Finally one's religious allegiance will shrink to something like a sports team loyalty, or having a favorite rock group. It will be like the household gods ancient people used to line up on the mantel.

In fact, we are already seeing the birth of non-sacred religions, religions that do not necessarily think of themselves *as* religions, such as the Elvis cult. A recent book analyzing the "Elvists" shrewdly recognizes that what is emerging in such cases is a religion that ignores the old distinction between the sacred and the secular. Alongside this, I would add that such pop culture religions ignore Kierkegaard's distinction between the ethical and the esthetic. There is no ultimate moral seriousness to the thing. It is a matter of firing the imagination, tickling the fancy. Morality may be as important as ever, but it need have nothing to do with religion.

Where will religion and religious symbols end up? Take a look at a catalog of Buddhist knick-knacks and yoga mats. I submit that such is the future of religion! A set of fashion accessories, mouse pads, ear rings, mood CDs, decor accents. Angel calendars. Angel movies. Eventually Jesus will be reduced to a Disney character on McDonald's glasses. He is already being edged out of Christmas by Ebenezer Scrooge.

Religion will be dead, or as good as dead. And then what will meet the needs of the human spirit?

In my opinion, worship is a set of special effects for inducing certain emotional and esthetic states. And the same states have long been induced in other ways, other esthetic means, like visual arts, music, poetry, drama. Care of the soul is already a matter of psychotherapy. Society already offers cultural rites of passage, though in our culture they have become attenuated. But graduations, "sweet sixteen" parties, weddings, and funerals are all still quite vital, with or without religious mythology.

We will still read the Bible. Why not? It is and never has been other than great myth, saga, epic, and poetry. The canon of scripture will be one with the canon of the great books of civilization. The imagination must be nourished, but one scarcely needs religious belief to do this. Rather, religious belief tends to put blinders on the free imagination.

So by losing religion we will not be losing much. Those of us who have lost it already can attest to that. And in that Great Noon we will have much to gain. We will gain sober realism, an ability to deem life much more precious for renouncing the illusion that we have an endless supply of it.

We will gain the glorious liberty of those who know they are not the sons or daughters of god, but only *Homo sapiens*, both beast and godling.

We will have the satisfaction of making our own decisions, no longer living for the goals and by the rules set by another.

We will not think glory lies in slavishly emulating ancient others of our kind, but in finding our own way.

We will admit the terrible truth of our own greatness and dare to bear the burden of it.

We will cower no longer, fearing we haven't the right to poach on God's prerogatives, since they are the prerogatives of our race— to clone ourselves, to reach out toward other planets, to extend life, to control the evolution of the race.

Dare to know! Dare to be your own god!

Because verily it is near to you: It is in your mouth and in your heart!

The Great Noon is at hand!

Notes

1. Trans. Walter Kaufmann (Baltimore: Penguin Books, 1978), p. 191.

Further Reading

Other titles available from Tellectual Press

Now that you've finished *Blaming Jesus for Jehovah*, here are some other titles you may wish to consider from Tellectual Press, (**tellectual.com**):

In ***Evolving out of Eden***, Dr. Price and co-author Edwin A. Suominen delve deep into the conflict that Chapter VIII summarized between religion and science. Writing with the combination of high criticism and low humor that fans have come to love from Dr. Price, they survey the apologetic landscape and offer a frank reckoning of evolution's significance for Christian belief. Religion originally provided the explanation for everything, they say in the book's concluding chapter, but now *it* is what requires so much explaining from its frustrated adherents.

Dr. Price applies his skepticism about the historicity of Jesus, touched on in Chapter VI, to another biblical figure in ***Moses and Minimalism***. The saga of Moses the Lawgiver, he says, is a mighty oak that has grown strong and thick through the centuries from an acorn of information found in the first five books of the Bible. But even the biblical Moses was the product of earlier stories, assembled by an unnamed, undated compiler.

Nor do the writings of Apostle Paul escape scrutiny under Dr. Price's examination of all things biblical: He is the editor of ***A Wave of Hypercriticism***, a collection of Willem Van Manen's English-language writings. Van Manen "began as a skeptic, eager to debunk and to refute" those few of his fellow countrymen who were questioning Paul's authorship of even the so-called "undisputed" epistles, says Dr. Price in his Introduction to the book. And the deeper he "delved into the issues and the arguments, the more he began to see their point and, worse yet, to suspect they were right." Van Manen was finally able to shrug off the shackles of pious obligation, directing himself, as he urged others in 1898, to undertake "free and impartial research as to the authenticity of the Pauline leading epistles."

If you're a Christian who is feeling a bit adrift after reading Dr. Price's take-down about about the less-than-perfect moral framework of Christianity, you might take a look at Charles Shingledecker's **Freedom to Doubt**. He accompanies fellow believers on an entertaining and informative journey through the Bible, Church history, and the nature of Christian belief.

For a bit of Bible-based fiction, check out Murray Sheehan's beautiful literary novel on the Garden of Eden story, **Eden**, originally published in 1928. It's a great retelling of the Genesis human-origins story, beautifully written and still very engaging to read nearly a century later. The Tellectual Press reprint includes an Introduction by Dr. Price and Edwin A. Suominen.

———

Each of these titles is available from Tellectual Press in both print and e-book format.

50252868R00094

Made in the USA
Lexington, KY
08 March 2016